THE VOICE

THE VOICE

Overcome Negative Self-Talk and
Discover Your Inner Wisdom

Dr. Brian Alman
with Dr. Stephen Montgomery

STERLING ETHOS
An imprint of Sterling Publishing Co., Inc.

New York / London
www.sterlingpublishing.com

Library of Congress Cataloging-in-Publication Data

Alman, Brian M. (Brian Mogul), 1950-
The voice : overcome negative self-talk and discover your inner wisdom /
Brian Alman, with Stephen Montgomery.
    p. cm.
ISBN 978-1-4027-7710-3
1. Self-talk. 2. Negativism. 3. Inner peace. 4. Wisdom. I. Montgomery,
Stephen, 1947-II. Title.
BF697.5.S47A46 2010
158.1--dc22

                                                         2010007963

10 9 8 7 6 5 4 3 2 1

Published by Sterling Publishing Co., Inc.
387 Park Avenue South, New York, NY 10016
© 2011 by Dr. Brian Alman
Distributed in Canada by Sterling Publishing
%o Canadian Manda Group, 165 Dufferin Street
Toronto, Ontario, Canada M6K 3H6
Distributed in the United Kingdom by GMC Distribution Services
Castle Place, 166 High Street, Lewes, East Sussex, England BN7 1XU
Distributed in Australia by Capricorn Link (Australia) Pty. Ltd.
P.O. Box 704, Windsor, NSW 2756, Australia

Sterling ISBN 978-1-4027-7710-3

For information about custom editions, special sales, premium and
corporate purchases, please contact Sterling Special Sales
Department at 800-805-5489 or specialsales@sterlingpublishing.com.

Contents

Finding Your Voice

The pain in my back was horrible. It disrupted my work, my play, my whole quality of life. What was going on with my back?

I knew my pain all too well. I was born without part of my lower back—specifically, part of the L4 and L5 vertebra—and I had been in some pain since I was old enough to walk. I had always been able to manage my pain with bed rest and medication, but it had been getting worse and worse in recent years. And now, at the age of twenty, it had become unbearable.

Hoping for answers, I consulted my orthopedic doctors in Boston. They advised me that to get any relief I would need a body cast for six months, then surgery, and then a body cast for another six months. This, they said, *might* alleviate *some* of the pain. But there were no guarantees. I might even be worse off after the procedures. Worst-case scenario? I might never walk again.

This wasn't what I wanted to hear. There *had* to be a better solution. Waiting, hurting, and worrying about the risks of surgery, I felt trapped in an impossible situation. Damned if I do, damned if I don't.

But mostly I was obsessed with these two burning questions: What was causing all this new pain? And what could I do about it?

The Wizard of Phoenix

My search for answers soon led me far from my home in Boston. Poring over medical journals in hopes of finding some help for my pain, I read about a physician in Phoenix, Arizona, Dr. Milton Erickson—known as "The Wizard of Phoenix"—who was a renowned master of mind-body healing. As a teenager Erickson had survived polio, but in mid-life the searing post-polio trauma in his muscles and joints had crippled him and left him wheelchair-bound. Faced with a life sentence of agonizing pain, Erickson decided to experiment on himself and see if he could find relief by using the power of his mind. And his experiment worked!

As described in the journals, this idea was startling to me, and full of promise. Maybe I had found my answer. If Dr. Erickson could manage his pain with his mind, why couldn't I? I wrote immediately and told him the history of my back pain. Dr. Erickson responded and generously invited me to come and study with him at his home in Phoenix.

But things didn't start out in a very promising fashion. The morning I met Dr. Erickson, he was frail and drained of energy, his eyes dull, his face contorted with pain—and I was, frankly, worried about his health. Was this drawn and ailing man slumped in a wheelchair the legendary healer I had read about? Had I come west on a wild goose chase?

Dr. Erickson asked to be excused, and then about an hour later I was astonished to see him wheel himself back into his study, fully alert and revitalized, cheery, eyes twinkling, ready to get to work.

What exactly was going on here? How could Dr. Erickson re-energize himself and bounce back in so short a time? Something truly wonderful had happened. Maybe it was no coincidence that Dr. Erickson had chosen to live in Phoenix, a city named for a mythical bird that dies in flames only to be reborn from its own ashes.

I was Dr. Erickson's patient and student for two years, learning how to alleviate my back pain, and also earning my PhD in psychology under his guidance. I was then what you might call a "co-therapist" with him for two more years, working with him on patients of my own. He shared his amazing insights and methods with me, not just for relieving pain, but also for dealing with any number of emotional challenges. The truth is, people can be hurting with physical pain or emotional pain—and often a combination of both—and Dr. Erickson and I discussed and treated many cases of each kind.

At the same time, Dr. Erickson encouraged me to continue my studies and develop my own ideas and techniques, both for my own therapy and for my patients. This respect for my ability to find my own best solutions was fundamental to Dr. Erickson's philosophy of healing, and was one of the most important lessons he taught me in our time together. In this and in so many ways, his tutelage and sensitivity were nothing less than inspiring.

Your Inner Doctor

But just as inspiring was Dr. Erickson's revolutionary insight into the healing process. He had pioneered the idea that to make positive changes in your life you need only look inside yourself and tap into your own rich inner resources. He once told me that in therapy "the patient's primary task is to develop his unconscious potential" and that healing is "something people receive from themselves." These statements have profound implications. They suggest that the power to heal resides not only in doctors and therapists, but in patients as well. They suggest, in other words, that you have what Albert Schweitzer called an "inner doctor" in your unconscious mind who can help you find your own best pathways to health and happiness.

In my study of meditation, I discovered that your "unconscious" or "inner doctor" was just another name for your inner wisdom, your inner guide, your inner Buddha, your intuition, your source, your soul, what the Irish poet W. B. Yeats described as your "deep heart's core," and what I like to call your "TruSage." This is your true, authentic inner voice, your voice of self-caring and self-healing, the voice of unconditional love that you've heard whispering in quiet moments, when it's not drowned out by all the loud negative voices in your head that clamor to create your life challenge.

What Dr. Erickson taught me about finding and connecting with this wise inner voice, and the healing process I've developed in my own practice over the last thirty years, helping thousands of patients with their physical and emotional challenges, is what I want to share with you in this book.

On Stress and Repression

Perhaps the first thing that Dr. Erickson taught me was the crucial role that emotional repression plays in stifling your voice and creating your personal challenge. The way Dr. Erickson put it, the body is the "receptacle" for repressed emotions, and when in times of stress you hold in your feelings, deny them, fight them, bury them, stuff them down into your body, you're sowing the seeds for serious physical and emotional problems.

Now we all have stress in our lives, and it's not always harmful. Stress can actually help us concentrate, focus, and perform our best in difficult situations. But the research clearly shows that the normal stresses and strains of daily life (what might be called "good" stress) can actually do great damage when we repress our feelings about our difficulties.

Think about that for a moment. It's not the difficulties themselves but our *repression of our feelings* that elevates our stress to dangerous levels.

In my years of study and practice, I've learned just what a pervasive problem stress is in people's lives. A 1994 Harvard study concludes that 60 to 90 percent of all doctor visits are stress related. Also, a 1997 study at Kaiser Permanente in San Diego, California, shows that the "chronic stress" caused by "adverse childhood experiences" ("ACE") in the family is far more prevalent than most medical doctors believe, and is highly correlated with a whole host of physical and emotional problems later in life, from obesity to alcoholism and depression. (I'll look more thoroughly at this powerful ACE study in the next chapter.) And, of course, every day in my practice I see a whole host of physical and emotional challenges caused by stress and repression.

When in Doubt, Dig Deeper

But my own life was my first and best example. Dr. Erickson would often tell me "When in doubt, dig deeper," and with his help I looked into my life, dug deep into my feelings, and (as I began listening to my healing inner voice) I came to understand that my back pain had become worse not because of some physical change, but because of the severe stress I was feeling about two seismic events that had violently shaken my family apart.

My pain first started to intensify in high school, right at the time when my parents were going through a divorce. Then, to make matters truly horrible, my mother contracted ALS (Lou Gehrig's Disease) and I watched her waste away in the prime of her life. All through these terrible years, I felt completely stressed-out, filled with anger, sadness, guilt, and frustration.

But I never let on. I tried to be the stoic New Englander and hold in my feelings. I wanted to be a grown-up about the divorce, and I wanted to be strong for my mother in her illness and not break down in tears all the time.

But now I know that my body paid the price. Not only did my back pain become intolerable, but also—and for the only time in my life—my weight shot up dramatically.

First, Things Happen on the Inside

So this was the answer to my first question: What was causing my pain? Clearly it was the stress and tension created by years of repressed feelings. Well and good. But just understanding this connection didn't answer my second question: What could I do about it?

This is the key question, and there is a general and a specific answer.

Let me start with the general answer. To get past your pain (physical or emotional), to reclaim your life, restore your confidence, and renew yourself, you need to learn how to listen to the powerful voice of your inner wisdom.

Wherever I teach seminars—and I've taught all over the United States, also in India, Germany, France, Holland, Japan, and many other countries—I like to begin by explaining that "first, things happen on the inside, and then they happen on the outside." This is just a simple way of saying that, if you want to make lasting improvements in your life—in your physical and emotional health, in your relationships, in your work and play—you really have to start on the inside, by improving the way you treat yourself.

By learning to care for yourself, to support yourself, to befriend yourself, even to love yourself—to be there for yourself, *no matter what*—you empower your inner voice and you make success in all areas of your life not only possible but inevitable.

And I'm living proof. In my case, once I began to recognize my feelings, to support myself, and to work positively with my physical and emotional pain, it was as if a load was lifted off my back. In just a few weeks—and to my amazement—I began to feel better. In six months, I was virtually pain free, and my weight was back to normal. It still seems like a miracle.

Working *with* Yourself

However, creating this new and healthier relationship with yourself isn't easy. Your physical and emotional challenges—not just body pain, but cravings and compulsions of all kinds (food, alcohol, cigarettes, sex), also fear, anxiety, anger, sadness, guilt, jealousy, grief, insomnia . . . the list goes on and on—can confront you daily, often many times a day, and they can get the better of you and rob you of your confidence and happiness. Singly or in combinations (food cravings combined with guilt, for example), these challenges attack your mind and body without warning, and for a time they take control of you.

So, again, how do you meet these complex challenges, discover the power of your inner voice, and heal your life?

The specific answer is you start working *with* yourself instead of *against* yourself by learning what I call the "Find Your Voice" process.

The Find Your Voice Process

The Find Your Voice process is based on the knowledge I've gathered about personal transformation in my thirty-year counseling career. This knowledge was gathered not only from Dr. Erickson, but also from many other gifted teachers around the world; gathered not just from my own experience as a patient and therapist, but also from my studies of meditation, self-hypnosis, NLP (Neuro-Linguistic Programming), The

Secret, and many other methods of self-help and mind-body healing.

It has taken me years to make this process simple, quick, and effective.

Here's how to deal successfully with any physical or emotional challenge. Spend just a few minutes a day, and as often as needed, taking yourself through the following three steps.

Step 1: Experience Your Challenge

First, stop trying to get rid of your challenge; that never works and is even counter-productive—the harder you try to fix yourself, the stronger your challenge becomes. Instead, begin to focus deliberately on the experience of your pain, craving, fear, sadness, and so forth. Let yourself become more fully *aware* of all your difficult thoughts, feelings, and sensations—everything that's part of your challenge. Then flow right into *accepting* your experience just as it is. And last, find some private way to *express* everything you're thinking and feeling—go ahead and say it all to yourself, write it down, act it out in your imagination. When you go deep inside and experience your challenge thoroughly and wholeheartedly, you learn what if feels like to be in touch with your true, authentic self, and this begins to empower the voice of your inner wisdom.

Step 2: Judge Your Challenge

Next, you need to deal constructively with your Inner Judge, that self-critical voice in your head that's quick to blame you and punish you for your mistakes and imperfections—even for being challenged at all. Poised in opposition to your true healing voice, your Inner Judge is the tireless voice of your social/family programming, and it's been drilled into you for so long that there's no getting rid of it. In fact, if you try to fight your Inner Judge, you only end up being more judgmental— you are, in effect, *judging* your Judge—and this only gives it energy. As in Step 1, the better way is to become *aware* of, to *accept*, and to *express* your Inner Judge. Only by embracing your Inner Judge and working *with* it can you relax this controlling, overanalyzing, never-satisfied, endlessly adversarial part of your mind.

Step 3: Resolve Your Challenge

Finally, as you experience and engage positively with all your pain and negativity—as you embrace all the thoughts, feelings, and self-criticisms that are driving your challenge—you find yourself spontaneously developing a new and more loving relationship with yourself. This new perspective on yourself naturally quiets the many strident voices of your challenge clashing in your mind, and almost immediately you begin to hear your true, authentic voice, your deep intuition, your TruSage. This voice is the real source of your healing power— it's where all your own best answers come from. And once you're able to listen to your voice, you quickly and effortlessly imagine creative ways of resolving your challenge. It's as if new ideas for health and happiness simply bubble up from your unconscious. And the more you listen, the more the craving, the pain, the fear—whatever your challenge—just dissolves away. It's really quite a miracle. And I don't use the word "miracle" very often.

That's all there is to it: 1-2-3. Each of the next three chapters will explain in detail *how to* accomplish these steps, offering a great many ideas, exercises, and techniques for getting in touch with your healing inner voice. In no time at all, you'll be moving quickly through the process, feeling confident that you can manage your challenge, instead of having it manage you.

Going to the Movies

To make the Find Your Voice process even easier to understand, here's a simple way of visualizing the three steps.

When dealing with a physical or emotional challenge, find a few minutes to be alone, get comfortable, take a couple of deep, satisfying let-go breaths, close your eyes, and picture yourself in a darkened movie theater, watching the movie of your life . . .

Step 1: On Screen

Up there on the big screen is the scene of your challenge. Maybe you're home alone; maybe you're at work, or with family or friends. Maybe you're in the midst of a craving or a wave of pain; maybe you're reliving a recent anxiety attack or an angry outburst. Whatever your challenge, just allow yourself to experience fully what's going on in your movie. Let the scene unfold; feel yourself acting your leading role, interacting with the other characters; hear yourself expressing everything, all your thoughts and feelings, just as they come to you.

Step 2: From the Fifteenth Row

After replaying the scene of your challenge, shift your attention and imagine yourself watching the scene from the fifteenth row of the theater, about halfway back. This is where your inner movie Critic sits, in the fifteenth row, and this skeptical, judgmental, perfectionist, controlling part of you is ready to tell you everything that's wrong with your movie and with yourself: "What's the matter with you?" . . . "Why can't you just stop it?" . . . "You know this won't work." Your Critic is too much a part of your inner life—it's been with you far too long—to be silenced. If you try to ignore, deny, or get rid of your Inner Critic (that is, if you're critical of your Critic), you only make it stronger, and you get yourself stuck in the fifteenth row. You're better off recognizing your Inner Critic, making friends with it, and letting it have its say.

Step 3: From the Last Row

Now, when you've finished beating yourself up, get up from your Critic's seat and move all the way back to the last row of the theater. From the last row, comfortably removed yet still involved, you can take a deep breath and begin to hear your true, authentic inner voice. From the last row, you can look at your movie more calmly and listen with more compassion to your fifteenth-row Inner Critic. From the last row, you can view your life with more love, more creativity, and with a wider, wiser perspective. And from the last row, you can regard your challenge no longer as a problem holding you back, but as a bridge to healing and evolving.

The Joy of Being *You*

By learning these three steps—experience your challenge, judge your challenge, and resolve your challenge—you'll quickly be able to connect with the healing voice of your inner wisdom. By mastering the Find Your Voice process, you'll soon feel the joy again of being *you*.

And you don't have to put it off. You don't have to wait for some age or event for this to happen. You know, you don't suddenly change inside because you turn thirty or forty or fifty or sixty or seventy or eighty or ninety—it's not an age thing. Things don't suddenly change inside because you go through a move or a divorce or a change in jobs or a graduation or a birth or a death.

Things *do* change because you decide you want to be happier and healthier. Things change because you decide you want to treat yourself like a person who's worthy and valuable. Things change because you find your voice and begin to say "Yes" to yourself.

It has to be a big "Yes"—a total, wholehearted "Yes!" Discovering your voice requires commitment, effort, care, time, energy, creativity, and love. It also requires courage—the courage to face your challenges, to embrace yourself, flaws and all, and to rediscover who you really are deep inside.

But once you gather your courage, make your commitment, and practice the Find Your Voice process for a time, you'll soon feel a shift and begin moving effortlessly into the real you. You'll begin to know what it feels like to be more centered, more relaxed, more confident, and more in harmony with life—to be in a beautiful flow that turns past problems into future successes. In spite of setbacks and slip-ups—these will happen—you'll begin feeling whole again, alive and well, and free to get on with your life.

As for me, it's been more than thirty years now since I

chose to learn about mind-body healing instead of submitting to back surgery. For almost all of that time, I've been 99 percent free of the pain that marred my childhood and then racked my teenage years. I'm able to run, work out, play tennis and golf, and travel around the world, helping people learn how to help themselves.

And, yes, I practice my own Find Your Voice process every day.

CHAPTER 1

Experience Your Challenge

he first principle of my Find Your Voice process is that
trying to fix yourself or get rid of your challenge just
doesn't work. In fact, the time and effort and money
you spend (on therapy, medication, seminars, and so on) trying
to get rid of your challenge only intensifies it. But doing just the
opposite—experiencing your challenge as fully as possible—
brings quick, spontaneous, and dramatic improvement.

My thirty years of study and my work with thousands of
patients (including myself) have convinced me of one thing:
The answer to your problem lies deep within the problem
itself, or, in other words, any problem can be a bridge to its
own solution. And so instead of more repression and struggle
against your challenge, you need to reverse course and begin to

embrace your problem wholeheartedly, (1) by becoming fully *aware* of what you're going through, (2) by *accepting* yourself just as you are, and (3) by *expressing* in safe, private ways all your most troubling thoughts and feelings.

No matter if you're dealing with pain, addiction, anxiety, anger, depression—any physical, emotional, or behavioral problem—the more completely you allow yourself to experience your challenge, the more you begin to hear the healing voice of your inner wisdom.

A Bad Case of the "Should's"

To illustrate my point, let me tell you about my client, Diane.

When Diane and I first talked in my office, I could tell right away she had a bad case of the "should's." Diane was suffering from severe anxiety attacks, and in these periods of near panic she was determined to fight off her alarming thoughts and feelings—those triggering her fears—and have only those she *should* have, those she approved of. She insisted, "I *should* only feel what I *should* feel and accept what I think *should* be acceptable." She firmly believed this was how to get free of her anxiety, how to "conquer my demon," as she put it. If only she could control her thoughts and feelings, and allow only the good positive ones, "then life would be wonderful," she said, "and I could move on."

Diane is a very intelligent person, but despite her best efforts to think and feel only what she *should*, she was getting nowhere—and she knew it. She described herself as "the hamster on the wheel," pedaling faster and faster, trying harder and harder, but just going around in circles. She even wondered if her "should's" were actually making matters worse: "The further I went with my cycle," she told me, "the further I fell into despair."

Like so many people I've worked with, Diane was trying her best to deal with a personal challenge, but was going about it in a counter-productive way. As I've said, fighting against your challenge, no matter how much self-control, willpower, or positive intention you bring to the task, just doesn't work. In fact, the energy you put into your fight only works against you.

Not to trivialize Diane's dilemma, but it was much like the Chinese finger puzzle—you know, the simple toy where you stick your index fingers into the ends of a small braided tube. The idea is to pull your fingers free, but the harder you try, the more the tube binds and traps you. To escape the trap, you have to do the opposite: You push your fingers gently *together* until the braid relaxes, and then you can slowly pull your fingers out.

Go with the Flow

While the Chinese finger puzzle is only child's play, the Pacific Ocean offers a far more powerful example of what I'm talking about.

I love swimming in the ocean near my home in Southern California, but I also know how dangerous it can be, particularly in winter, when storm surges push in very high tides. Sometimes, when the waves get really big and gouge wide trenches in the ocean floor, powerful riptides form under the surface of the water and pull strongly out to sea. Most beaches in the area have a few very difficult spots like this where every year swimmers get caught in rip currents and are sucked out from shore. Many of these people have to be saved by the lifeguards, and a few people drown.

The problem is that most people's instinct when caught in a riptide is to swim against it. But this hardly ever works. Usually the rip current is so powerful that it goes on sucking you out farther and deeper. You fight and fight to get out of it, but your energy isn't enough. Then, by fighting so hard, you become completely exhausted . . . and things can get worse and worse.

Not many people know how to spot a riptide in the surf, and even fewer know how to get out of one. Here's a simple technique—many people are surprised by how simple—that lifeguards teach people to deal with riptides.

When you realize you're caught in a riptide, don't panic and fight against it, but go with it, ride with it—even swim along with it—and you'll soon come out of it without any trouble.

You see, the rip current is stronger in the shallow water near the shore, and then it becomes weaker farther out in deep water. At the very end, at the farthest point, it's so weak that you're simply out of it. You don't need to *struggle* to get out of it; you're simply out of it. Then you just swim to the side until you're clear of the current, and make your way back in to shore.

This is a wonderful lesson from the ocean that you can remember when you're dealing with any physical or emotional challenge. Instead of fighting your inner riptide and drowning in your thoughts and feelings, you can choose to "go with the flow."

Thus, if you feel afraid, or sad, or angry, or like bingeing, or are in pain—anything at all—simply dive into your feeling and you'll find that you quickly come out of it. In a few minutes, your feeling will simply be gone. If you dive deep into it and ride with it, you're soon out of it, and recharged, not exhausted, because you weren't fighting with it. There was no question of fighting or resisting. You weren't pretending that you didn't have the feeling. You weren't repressing the feeling to avoid dealing with it. You let yourself experience the feeling fully and wholeheartedly, and in no time at all the feeling just weakened of itself and disappeared, and you can hardly remember what it was. You're soon going on about your day wondering what all the fuss was about.

Explore the Starting Point

The big waves that pound out riptides have their origin thousands of miles away in mid-ocean. Similarly, our inner riptides have a distant origin, usually in much earlier life experiences. In almost all cases, our adult challenges begin in childhood or adolescence, sometimes in traumatic events, but most often in disturbing and chronic family patterns that we've been avoiding, denying, repressing, or ignoring for years or decades.

What this means is that any full experience of your current challenge needs to include an exploration of the starting point, those stressful episodes in your childhood that might well be at the bottom of your craving, anxiety, fear, pain, despondency, and so forth. Put another way, watching the movie of your challenge is a much more complete experience when you can explore through flashbacks (or a "back story") the scene of how, when, and where all the trouble began.

But before you begin, here are some important ideas to keep in mind:

❶ Set your goal in writing. Start keeping a Find Your Voice journal and write down for yourself, "I want to better understand why I began to . . . ." The goal should be specific (for example, "to overeat," "to feel afraid," "to drink," "to have back pain," and so on) and it should be open to all possibilities.

❷ Be aware that you're dealing with issues that are hard to face. Be aware of the challenge; don't pretend and live in a state of denial. Allow yourself to consider any issues that may come up for you. Encouraging your own openness to hidden material may lead you to find options that can help you break down conscious resistance to change.

❸ Try to notice when you feel yourself closing in on an important issue. Pause for a moment and review it privately in your mind. Talk to yourself (out loud or silently), and write down any words and ideas that can help you understand more about any issues that seem significant. This is giving your wise inner voice a chance to be heard.

❹ Make this work of self-awareness a priority. Make a commitment to plan a schedule for inner exploration—once a day, twice a day, or whatever time you can devote. You decide how often and how long you can spend on this, respecting your wish to make a significant change in your life.

The ACE Study

To help you get started, answer the following questionnaire, which was devised by Vincent J. Felitti, MD, and Robert F. Anda, MD, as part of the Adverse Childhood Experiences (ACE) Study that I mentioned in the Introduction. Take your time and give each answer some careful thought.

WHAT'S YOUR ACE SCORE?

Prior to your eighteenth birthday:

1. Did a parent or other adult in the household *often or very often...*

> Swear at you, insult you, put you down, or humiliate you?
>
> *or*
>
> Act in a way that made you afraid that you might be physically hurt?

Yes   No   If yes, enter 1 _____

2. Did a parent or other adult in the household *often or very often...*

> Push, grab, slap, or throw something at you?
>
> *or*
>
> *Ever* hit you so hard that you had marks or were injured?

Yes   No   If yes, enter 1 _____

3. Did an adult or person at least five years older than you *ever...*

> Touch or fondle you or have you touch their body in a sexual way?
>
> *or*
>
> Attempt or actually have oral, anal, or vaginal intercourse with you?

Yes   No   If yes, enter 1 _____

4. Did you *often* or *very often* feel that...

> No one in your family loved you or thought you were important or special?
>
> *or*
>
> Your family didn't look out for each other, feel close to each other, or support each other?

Yes   No   If yes, enter 1 _____

5. Did you *often* or *very often* feel that . . .

> You didn't have enough to eat, had to wear dirty clothes, and had no one to protect you?
>
> *or*
>
> Your parents were too drunk or high to take care of you and take you to the doctor if you needed it?
>
> Yes   No   If yes, enter 1 _____

6. Was a biological parent *ever* lost to you through divorce, abandonment, or other reason?

> Yes   No   If yes, enter 1 _____

7. Was your mother or stepmother:

> *Often* or *very often* pushed, grabbed, slapped, or had something thrown at her?
>
> *or*
>
> *Sometimes, often, or very often* kicked, bitten, hit with a fist, or hit with something hard?
>
> *or*
>
> *Ever* repeatedly hit over at least a few minutes or threatened with a gun or knife?
>
> Yes   No   If yes, enter 1 _____

8. Did you live with anyone who was a problem drinker or alcoholic, or who used street drugs?

> Yes   No   If yes, enter 1 _____

9. Was a household member depressed or mentally ill, or did a household member attempt suicide?

> Yes   No   If yes, enter 1 _____

10. Did a household member go to prison?

Yes   No   If yes, enter 1 _____

Now add up your "Yes" answers: _____
This is your ACE score.

If you have some "Yes" answers, don't be surprised—you aren't alone. The startling results of the ACE Study were that of the 17,000 solidly middle-class, racially balanced participants, nearly *two-thirds* had an ACE score of 2 or more, and one in six had a score of 4 or more! These findings suggest that the incidence of childhood abuse, family dysfunction, and parental neglect is much higher than generally recognized by the medical community, most likely (say the authors) because such difficult issues are often hidden "by time, by shame, by secrecy, and by social taboos."

And the effects of such repressed early life trauma were staggering. Decades later, the participants were still seeking relief by engaging in compulsive coping behaviors such as overeating, smoking, alcoholism, illicit drug use, and sexual promiscuity. Moreover, the higher the ACE score, the stronger the relationship to emotional problems like depression, amnesia, and hallucinations; and the same was true for medical disorders such as liver disease, heart disease, coronary artery disease, and autoimmune disease.

Dr. Felitti and Dr. Anda's conclusion was inescapable: "All told it is clear that adverse childhood experiences have a profound, proportionate, and long-lasting effect" on people's physical and emotional problems.

Try to Remember

The ACE Study questionnaire can put you in touch with your childhood memories, but here's a Find Your Voice exercise that can take you deeper. Find a quiet, private place to spend a few minutes, sit in a comfortable chair, take some deep, relaxing breaths, and let yourself sink into memory...

Try to remember a happy and healthy time in your life when your challenge wasn't an issue in your life. Let your memory take you back to that time before your problem began. If you can, go over an entire day in your mind's eye (or on your inner movie screen), from getting up in the morning to going to bed at night. Remember as many details as possible.

Next, try to remember an unhappy and unhealthy time when you first experienced your challenge. Be honest about your feelings and go over the incident step by step. Whatever the memory might be, try to picture the scene in as much detail as you can. Play the scene on your inner movie screen, and be yourself as a child, see the other people involved, hear all their voices, feel all the feelings as fully as possible. Don't try to control the flow of memory, but dive deep into it and let it take you where it will. If your mind drifts, go with it; mental side trips can be more valuable than you think.

You might ask yourself, "Is there some past event responsible for my challenge? Was it before I was twenty years old? Was it before I was ten years old? Was it before I was five years old?"

Try to recall what was going on in your life at the time, especially in your family. Try to remember details. When you know what it was, you'll relax, and you'll be able to describe it to yourself or write it down in your journal.

You might ask yourself, "Is it all right to tell myself about this?"

You might ask yourself, "Is there an earlier experience that might have set the stage or made me vulnerable to my challenge?"

You might ask yourself, "Is there anything else I need to know before I can feel free of the problem?"

You might ask yourself, "Now that I know this, can I be well?"

You'll probably need to work with your memories several times before you begin to see results. Be patient and listen to your unconscious mind—it speaks in your true, authentic voice. When it's ready, it will tell you all you need to know about when to expect a change in your life.

Unfinished Business

When I was a kid, people said that "Time heals all wounds." And today people say, "Get over it!" Well, I'm afraid that just doesn't happen very easily for most of us. I've worked with many, many elderly people, people in their eighties, and they're still struggling with hurtful things that happened to them in childhood. They've gotten on with their lives, one way or another, but they still have old wounds that haven't healed properly and are causing them trouble. In other words, they still have unfinished business to deal with, and as long as it's unfinished, it continues to cause them inner conflict and stress, and to create challenges for them.

Now, it's sad but true that most of our unfinished business has to do with our parents. I hate to pick on parents—I'm a parent myself—but our feelings toward our parents (or toward anyone who raised us) are usually a mixture of love and resentment. After all, our mother and/or father were our primary source of love, support, and security, but they were also our primary source of punishment, criticism, fear, guilt, and restriction. Our relationship with them is therefore almost always filled with positives and negatives, with gratitude and with regret, with caring and with anger, with sweet memories and with bitter. This is why we have such a sense of conflict about our parents, or parental figures, and why we often repress our feelings about them.

So, if you want to finish with all your old business, get it done with and then move on in life, you simply have to settle some things with your parents. To get healthy in your relationship with yourself, you need to become aware of the hurts you've received from your parents, and to understand how deeply you've buried your thoughts and feelings about them. And then you need to really let go and get some things off your chest.

No blaming here, no staying stuck in the past. We know our parents had parents themselves, and the issues have probably been going on for generations. This is all about expressing and moving forward.

Let It All Go

Here's a Find Your Voice exercise that lets you express your thoughts and feelings for your parents in a safe and freeing way. Get yourself comfortable, breathe deeply, maybe stretch your arms and legs, and . . .

Picture yourself sitting in your inner theater, only this time you're watching a play about your life. Now whenever you're ready, I want you to imagine that you get up and walk down the aisle, and then up the steps on the side, and onto the stage, and then right into the play. That's right—you walk right into the play about your life.

And when you enter the set, you see that either one or both of your parents are in the scene with you. But now you're in charge. You organize the set the way you want it. You can be sitting or standing. Your parents or parent can be on the other side of the stage or close by. It's up to you. You design the set. You direct the movement. You make it any way you want it, the way you're most comfortable.

Now, I want you to imagine saying exactly what you think and feel to your parents. Speak to them honestly about the way they treated you, about how they hurt you while you were growing up: "This went on for years and years and years, from the time I was four until I was nineteen, and the only reason it stopped then was because I moved out!" Really, let it all go.

Express whatever you feel about the way they treated you, and as you're saying it, I want you to write it all down in your journal, with your non-dominant hand. Why your non-dominant hand? Because this will help you break out of your lifelong family programming and respond more freely, creatively, intuitively—in your true, authentic voice—as if you were a child again just learning how to write.

Here's your opportunity. No more holding back. No more pushing down. Take this opportunity to let go, to express, to release whatever you feel toward your parents or parent. Speaking, shouting, screaming, scribbling, doodling, writing words, expressing thoughts and feelings. From your heart to your head to your hand.

This is your opportunity right now to say whatever you want to say, whatever you've been holding back, whatever you've never said but knew you wanted to say. Years of feelings, maybe decades of feelings, and you can now tell your parents how they've affected your life, what they've done to your life, what they've done to your self-esteem and self-confidence.

If it's sad, let it be sad. If it's angry, let it be angry. If it's intense, let it be intense. If it's simple, let it be simple. If it's exactly what you thought you felt, wonderful. If it's different from what you thought you felt, now that you're saying it, fine. It's all about you expressing, releasing, letting go.

No more holding back now, thinking things like "A good son or daughter wouldn't feel this way" or "A nice person wouldn't have reacted the way I've reacted," because that's what caused all the stress, and all the repression, and all the difficulty in the first place. You hold it in with all these judgments about yourself. So my advice is, say it all, and let it all go.

Once and for all, let it all go. Out of you directly to your parent or parents and onto the paper, released out of your mind, out of your body, out of your gut, out of your back, out of the spaces where you've been holding it all these years (and you know where those spaces are). Free yourself up. Stop using your strength to hold it in. Get it out so you can use your strength for healthier and better things in your life from this day forward. This is the path to freedom. This is the path to healing.

Okay. Now when you're ready, here comes one of the most important questions, a healing question, a very powerful question that you need to go deep inside to answer. And watch what a difference this makes in how you feel forever about your unfinished business and about your parents.

Here's the question: What do you want your parents or parent now to say back to you? And with your non-dominant hand and just allowing it to move across the paper, what do you want—after expressing all this, saying all this, letting go of all this, being real, being total, being 100 percent—what do you want your parent or parents now to say back to you? A sentence, a word, more, less, I don't know. Go ahead and write it down. What do you want your parents or parent to say back to you?

The beautiful thing about this technique is that you don't ever have to confront your parents in person. You say it all, let it go, and finish with it for yourself, in your own imagination, in a safe and healing and empowering way—and then you're done with it. You resolve it on your own and really get free of all your repressed thoughts and feelings. Then when you're with your parents, if they're still alive and still a part of your life, you have this compassionate last-row perspective on them that is wonderful.

Tree Rings

The Find Your Voice memory exercises that you've done so far will help you get free of your past, but let me caution you that it's no good thinking you can get *rid* of your past. Good or bad, happy or sad, your past is with you always, an ingrained part of you. To use another metaphor from nature, it's like tree rings, the growth rings inside a tree that reflect each year's rainfall. In any tree's life, there are wet years and dry years, and so some of its rings are narrow and some are wide.

Now, if a tree isn't doing well, you can't cut it down and carve out the narrow rings for the difficult years, and then stick it back together and expect it to live. Narrow or wide, those rings have been an integral part of the tree's growth and development. They *are* the tree.

Well, you are like a tree in this sense: You can't change the experiences in your past. For better or worse, they're with you all the way.

But what you can do is become aware of your past, accept it, express it, and learn from it how to take better care of yourself now and in the future.

With Every Breath You Take

Exploring your past, and hearing again the hurtful voices that are part of your past, can help you heal old wounds and make possible a brighter future. But you mustn't dwell in the past, or live in the future, and lose sight of the fact that your life happens right here, right now, moment by moment. The more fully you can experience your challenge right now—the more you can dive into your challenge and swim with it—the happier you'll feel, the more freedom you'll feel.

The best way to start "going with the flow" of your challenge in the present moment is to focus on the flow of your breathing.

Breathing might seem insignificant; in fact, most people ignore their breathing, have almost no awareness of it, and hardly even know it's there. And yet it can be invaluable in helping you experience your challenge. Your breathing mirrors your inner life; if you learn to pay attention to your breathing, you'll begin to recognize the automatic pattern of your challenge and of your social/family programming, and this will weaken its power over you.

Observe your breathing over a day or two; pay particular attention during your times of challenge. If your breathing tends to be quick and shallow (short, rapid breaths, stomach held a little tight), that's a sure sign that you're struggling to control your thoughts and hold in your feelings. This is your repressed and stressful breathing.

Here's what to do: Don't do anything. Trying to change your breathing will only cause more struggle and stress. That's your Inner Judge trying to take over and make things perfect.

Instead, for now, just become aware of your breathing as it is. Just listen to the voice of your breathing. At the same time, let yourself accept the flow of your breathing. Recognize that word, "accept." Accept your breathing just as it is. Simply ride with the rise and fall of each breath and accept your breathing as it is.

The truth is it really doesn't matter if your breathing is quick and shallow, or slow and deep, if it's nose or mouth breathing or abdominal or chest breathing. What does matter is that when you're feeling stressed, you pause and take a minute to observe your breathing. There's nothing you need to do right, nothing you can do wrong. Just observe and accept your breathing as it comes and goes, like watching the waves at the beach coming in and going out. Small and choppy, or long and rolling, it really doesn't matter.

As you practice observing your breathing—feeling the rise and fall of each breath—you are naturally, little by little, learning to relax into deeper awareness and acceptance of your thoughts and feelings, and of your true, authentic voice. And this is the beginning of transformation.

Turning Points

Most people don't know that breathing has four parts to it. There are the inhale and the exhale, of course, but as each breath rises and falls, at the very bottom and top of the breathing cycle, there are also turning points. They're the moments when your inhale turns into your exhale, and then when your exhale turns into your inhale. These turning points are in every breath you've ever taken, ever will take. They last only a split-second. They're a transition, and a fusion.

As you observe your breathing, notice when your turning points come, how long they last, and when they begin to turn. You might focus on the bottom of your exhale as the root of your breathing, or you might focus on the top of your inhale as the crown of your cycle. And you might focus even more closely and see that there's the tiniest pause in the middle of each turning point, a millisecond of profound silence poised between your inhales and your exhales.

By observing, listening to, and accepting these turning points, giving them your full attention, you begin to make space in your awareness for your inner voice to be heard. The effects can be positive, centering, and calming. As you relax your body and mind, you may find yourself becoming more aware of your stress, of your social/family programming, and of yourself as a whole person. You may find that the voice of your challenge—your pain, fear, anger, craving, and so on—begins to fade and seem separate from you. And you may start to trust that, like the turning point in each breath, you'll always be able to get through your challenge and feel a sense of renewal.

So, whenever you find yourself dealing with a difficulty, challenge, or stressful moment, just use your breathing as a bridge. Within a few moments, you can shift from tense to relaxed, from negative to positive, from problem to solution. Observe your breathing as it is, focus on the cycle, accept the turning points, and you'll soon be in a beautiful, relaxed, healthy, comfortable state, having transcended your stresses and troubles.

Say Your Name

Here's a Find Your Voice breathing exercise that can further enhance your awareness and acceptance of your challenge. I learned this simple technique from a remarkable woman I met when I was on a teaching and learning tour in India. This woman had been a humble housekeeper all her life, but in her sixties she realized she had healing powers, so she quit her job, took up her calling, and within a few years she had become one of the most sought-after healers in all of India. When I asked her if she would share with me her favorite technique, she told me about "Say Your Name." It was her gift to me, and now I'm giving it to you.

When you're feeling in the grip of your challenge, caught up in your anxiety, anger, sadness, pain, and so on, pause for a moment and focus on your breathing. Even if your breathing is tight, shallow, and stressful, just observe your inhale and exhale, maybe notice the turning points—just simply focusing . . . inhale and then exhale.

After a few breaths, on an exhale, say your name to yourself, but not out loud, just say your own name. First name, last name, full name, nickname—whatever favorite name you use when you talk to yourself. Just inhale, pause, and on the exhale, say your name to yourself, and continue doing this for several breaths.

Once you're in a nice rhythm, on an inhale, say silently, "I accept" . . . or "I support" . . . or "I care about" . . . or even "I love," and then pause, and on the exhale, say your name. Do this for a minute (or for ten to fifteen breaths). Make it a kind of silent mantra of unconditional acceptance of yourself and your challenge. You're speaking in the healing voice of your inner TruSage.

Give this wonderful healer's technique some time and energy, and watch what happens. You'll be amazed to find yourself feeling more relaxed and accepting of what you're going through with your challenge.

You'll want to practice this whenever you have the chance. This will just get better and better for you. This is a gold medal winner.

Breathing Colors

You can make breathing for acceptance and expression even more effective by switching this part of your movie into Technicolor.

When you're in the grip of your challenge, try to identify what color you're feeling inside. That's right, what *color*. You might not have thought about it, but many of our negative thoughts, feelings, and moods are associated with colors. When we're angry, we "see red." If we're afraid, we're called "yellow." We can be "green" with envy. When we're sad, we feel "blue." We can be in a "black mood" or a "brown study." Your challenge color might be one of these, or any other color you sense about your inner atmosphere. It might be a solid color or a combination of colors. It might be a block of color or a swirl. You decide.

Now as you take some slow, full breaths, imagine your breath going everywhere in your body, from your head to your toes, circulating, moving, gathering up all the color (or colors) in your head, in your stomach, in your muscles, in your cells—and then you exhale fully and watch the color flow from you and spread, disperse, and vanish into thin air.

You might think of the clear fresh air you inhale as a cleaner working inside of you—maybe one of those "activated oxygen" cleaners you see advertised. You breathe it in, and let it go everywhere, absorbing your color, soaking up your stress, and then you breathe it out. And then it's gone, out of you, and along with it, much of your troubled mood or mindset.

Out of Sight Is Not Out of Mind

Working with your breath can do wonders in a moment of challenge, but working directly with the challenge itself is even more powerful. And the best thing to do with your challenge is to become more fully aware of exactly what's happening.

Awareness of your challenge is so important because most of us spend most of our lives in a state of unawareness. As I've said, early in life we learn to repress our emotions, to stuff down our desires, our anger, our fear—whatever causes us too much trouble, or puts too much stress on our family. And this seems to work; this seems to solve the problem. Pretty soon, with all this repressing, we just become unconscious of these troubling thoughts and feelings; we start forgetting about them, and we don't even think they exist anymore.

But they don't disappear. Out of sight is not out of mind. In fact, these repressed thoughts and feelings go down deep inside and grow strong in hiding, and they begin to exert a kind of silent, subversive control over you, taking their revenge by causing all sorts of physical and emotional problems.

A healthier and more effective way of dealing with your challenge is to bring your thoughts and feelings back into consciousness, into full awareness. Now this can be hard because most of us have been repressing for so long that we don't know any other way. Repression feels natural to us. It may even feel *right* to us. But this isn't how we're made to work. Ignoring, denying, stuffing down our thoughts and feelings always eventually causes problems. Sooner or later, ignorance stops being bliss.

Restoring your awareness is the first step in the right direction.

Three Times Is the Charm

Try this simple Find Your Voice technique to help you increase your awareness of your challenge.

When any challenge comes up for you—an urge, a craving, pain, anger, fear, anything that troubles you—just be aware of it, just notice that it's there inside of you, and name it slowly three times. For example, if it's a craving, just notice it and say to yourself, "Craving . . . craving . . . craving," or go ahead and say what it is you're craving. For instance, "Chocolate . . . chocolate . . . chocolate." Or let's say you're angry about something, someone, yourself, others, the situation, anything—just recognize it and say, "Anger . . . anger . . . anger." Say it out loud or at least to yourself. Say it slowly three times. You'll find yourself naturally shifting into your true, authentic voice.

Don't miss a single opportunity. Whenever you feel burdened by any thoughts, or any feelings, or any cravings— even anger, even fear, even worry, even pain—just note it three times, whatever it is. "Fear . . . fear . . . fear." "Worry . . . worry . . . worry." "Pain . . . pain . . . pain." Say it slowly three times, and watch what happens. It's very, very beautiful how when you find your healing voice, you naturally begin to let your challenge go.

Is there something magical about three times? Well, maybe, but what's important is that, by saying it three times, you become more aware of your challenge, more present with it. And once you become more aware of it—and you don't do anything else, except say it three times—an amazing thing happens: Your challenge loses its power. Once you're aware of it inside, you become separate from it, and soon here you are in the present, just watching it, just noticing it.

But it's important to say your challenge out loud or at least to yourself three times, because by saying it three times, and making it absolutely conscious, being very aware of it, and being very focused on it, the trouble melts away.

Focus on Your Body

Increasing your body awareness is also a key part of experiencing your challenge. Recent research in Germany has shown clearly that when you're able to focus on your body and your physical sensations, you deal with both physical and emotional problems much more quickly and effectively.

Loss of body awareness, on the other hand, is an essential part of locking in your challenge. When you get caught up in your head—in your inner arguments and emotional turmoil—you lose touch for the moment with your sure grounding in physical reality. You feel out of your body, off-center, literally "beside" yourself with your pain, craving, fear, anger, and so forth.

But with greater body awareness, you feel more present in your own skin, more whole and alive, and much more able to connect with your voice.

Feel Your Pain

For instance, if you're in pain, don't fight your pain and try to get rid of it—that will only create more stress and make the pain worse. Instead (and though this might seem counterintuitive), do the opposite:

Dive deep into your pain and experience it as fully as possible. Focus on your pain, concentrate on your pain, and study your pain. Examine your pain thoroughly. Describe it to yourself. Give it dimension, shape, texture, and even taste. Imagine it as a physical object, or perceive the temperature of your pain. Is it a burning sensation? Is it like a hot poker in your back? Does it feel as if hot oil is spreading over your shoulder? Does your head throb with the pulsing of your heart? Is it like needles stabbing your foot?

The more vividly you can describe your pain—the more physically you can feel your pain—the sooner you'll be able to relax and let it go.

Watch What You Eat

Or let's say that your challenge is overeating. If you struggle with this, you already know that using willpower to stop yourself from eating too much just doesn't work. A better way to curb your craving for food is to use awareness instead—to "watch" what you eat.

The next time you sit down to a meal, maybe your favorite meal, your favorite food, anything you want, imagine you're eating this food for the first time. Watch the scene closely; observe yourself as you eat. Notice your mood, your attitude, how tense or relaxed you are. Observe your breathing, shallow or deep. Watch how you hold your knife and fork.

Watch as you raise the food to your nose and smell the aromas. Look at your food closely. What shape is it? How many shades of color does it have? Watch the food as it goes into your mouth—but don't chew it yet. Just move it around in your mouth. Can you notice different flavors in different parts of your mouth? Now, chew it and listen. What can you hear? Crackling, swishing, crunching? Are the sounds coming from the food or from inside you? What texture does the food have? Grainy, spongy, crisp? How hot or cold is it? What aftertaste does it leave? Be aware as the food goes into your stomach. Is your stomach happy to receive it?

The amazing thing is that just by becoming more aware of your eating, not trying to control it, not trying to change a thing, your eating will change by itself. By making the physical act of eating 100 percent of your focus, you'll find that you stop eating when your food stops tasting good. You'll forget cleaning your plate. You'll forget three meals a day. You'll be aware of what your body tells you in your true, authentic voice, and when you're no longer hungry, you'll stop eating.

Give Your Tension Some Attention

Becoming more fully aware of your body in moments of challenge also has this great advantage: It allows you to become more aware of the tension you're holding inside.

We all carry around a certain amount of muscle tension to help us get through the ordinary challenges of daily life. But as I explained in the Introduction, tension builds to excessive, unhealthy levels when you have a fight going on inside, a fight (usually started by your Inner Judge) to deny or to repress your perfectly natural thoughts and feelings.

Your Inner Judge wants to control your spontaneity, keeping you safe within the familiar boundaries of your social/family programming—it is suspicious of change and is actually trying to protect you!—and so it fights long and hard to stop you from having thoughts and feelings that it finds threatening or unacceptable. Such thoughts are usually just a tiny part of your movie, but your Inner Critic wants to censor them and cut them out of your life script entirely and forever. As these two sides square off—your on-screen self and your fifteenth-row Critic—your muscles tense for the struggle.

What to do? Again, at this point, you needn't do anything. Just give your tension some attention.

Speaking to Your Body

Just as pain is a message from your body that you've damaged yourself, so muscle tension is a message from your body that you're fighting yourself. If you ignore this message, tension will coil inside you almost without your knowing it, winding you up more and more tightly in your challenge. But by becoming more aware of your tension, you can stop the fight and feel better in seconds.

When you're feeling stressed and challenged, and you can find a moment alone, simply focus on your tension. Feel the tension in your whole body. Try to rate your tension on a scale of 1 to 10, with

1 being fully relaxed and 10 being really stressed out. What's your level of tension right now?

Next, turn your attention to your breathing, maybe observe your turning points, and when you're ready, close your eyes and say the following three lines to your body out loud (but softly): "Thank you for working so well for me all these years. I'm sorry if I've been ignoring you. If there's anything that you're trying to tell me, I'm totally open right now."

Go ahead and scan your body from head to toe, looking for knots of tension or stress. Most of us have special areas where we hold our tension, often in the eyes or jaw, in the neck or shoulders, or in the stomach or lower back. Now, repeat these lines, say them aloud again, while you focus on that part of your body where there's tension or tightness: "Thank you for working so well for me all these years. I'm sorry if I've been ignoring you. If there's anything you're trying to tell me, I'm totally open right now."

If you feel your tension hanging on tightly, it helps to get in touch with your body. So this time, focus on an area of your body where you feel extra tension, or stress, or worry, or pain. Wherever the tension or stress is, place one of your hands directly on that spot. That's right, actually lift your hand up and put it right on the place of tension. Now with very light pressure, rub the area with your fingertips in a counter-clockwise motion, and once again say these words aloud, but softly, and directly to the area: "Thank you for working so well for me all these years. I'm sorry if I've been ignoring you. If there's anything you're trying to tell me, I'm totally open right now."

After scanning for tension and repeating these three lines at least three times, rate your tension again on a scale of 1 to 10. How are you feeling now? Most people report a drop of three or four points the first time they try this exercise. And it only gets better with practice.

Make sure you don't try to change or relax your tension; just notice where it lives and what it feels like. You're speaking to your body—and it will answer—in your true, authentic voice.

Entrance and Exit

Your objective in all of these exercises is to experience your challenge as fully as possible. Here's another Find Your Voice technique that offers a remarkable "in the body" experience. It will help you dive into your tension and go with the flow. Dr. Milton Erickson developed this technique—which he called "Entrance and Exit"—to help relieve his debilitating pain, and I've used it in my own Find Your Voice practice ever since.

When you feel your tension building, start by focusing on your breathing—inhale . . . exhale. You might think of your breathing now as an entrance—that's the inhale—and as an exit—that's the exhale. Entrance . . . exit. That's right, stay with the flow, get into a little routine.

Now, on an inhale, dive right into your tension. Squeeze your muscles tight and feel the tension—exaggerate the tension—in your whole body, from top to bottom. Tense your feet. Grip your hands into fists. Shut your eyes tight. Clench your jaw. Lift your shoulders up. Tighten your stomach. Squeeze your buttocks and your thighs. Hold the tension just as long as you can—feel your whole body tense, tense, tense. And then exhale, releasing and really relaxing, everything open, everything loose, like a rag doll.

Good, you're going to do this again. Bring the tension in with your breath and really get into it. Squeeze everything, your hands, your eyes, your mouth, your feet, your legs, and your belly— squeeze them all; feel the tightness everywhere. Lift your shoulders up toward the top of your head, and tense your back and buttocks. When you're ready, when you can't hold it any longer, exhale and release. So you enter into your tension—feel every bit of it—and then you get free. Entrance . . . exit.

One more time, inhale and squeeze your body, everything, and get as tense as you can, shoulders up, fists clenched, feet, belly, jaws, everything. Hold it as long as possible, a little bit longer than last time, experience your tension fully, and then release it all as you exhale. What a difference.

Beautiful. You're going to find that after practicing Entrance and Exit for a few weeks, you'll automatically relax anytime you start to feel stressed, worried, tense, or in some discomfort. It will become a new part of your programming.

Stress and relaxation, inhale and exhale, entrance and exit. That's a present from Dr. Erickson to me, and to you.

The Mind Monkey

The inner battle that tenses up your breathing and your body also rages in your mind. For most people, the mind under stress is a jumble of voices, thoughts, and feelings, changing every moment. It's like a choir with each member singing a different song in a different key. It's like trying to watch television, listen to your iPod, and read text messages all at the same time.

One moment you're filled with doubt about ever getting through your challenge, and the next moment you feel hopeful—then wait a minute and you're doubtful again. One moment you're committed to being healthy and happy, and the next moment you feel adrift and lost. One moment you're loving toward yourself and others, and then the wheel turns and you're full of frustration and criticism.

One client, Cheryl, told me that when she was trying "not to be so tense," she couldn't "stop her head from chattering." Another client, Barry, used exactly the same word: He told me that his mind kept "chattering" when he was trying hard "not to be angry."

In Buddhism, this is called the "Mind Monkey," which chatters and shrieks as it swings in your head from thought to thought to thought. But to me, this mind chatter is more like a room full of monkeys. To me, it's like an out-of-control committee meeting with all your various inner committee members—all the strident voices in your head—talking at the same time, arguing with each other, trying to outwit or just out-scream each other, trying to hold the floor and dominate each other.

Sitting around the conference table are all your usual committee members: Anger, Fear, Sadness, Frustration, and Guilt. The list can go on and on. Everyone's committee is unique, but we all seem to have a lot in common, too. You might have given Willpower a seat on the committee, or Self-Doubt, or Hope, or Failure, or Why Me? Other familiar voices might clamor to be heard: your Inner Child, your Inner Parent, your I Should Be Perfect self, or your What's the Matter with Me? self. You might have only three or four committee members, or you might have more than a dozen—

all representing different thoughts and feelings fighting it out in your head.

Vince's Voices

Let me tell you about Vince, a client of mine who was battling food cravings and trying to lose a lot of weight. Vince called the voices in his head concerning his weight problem "dysfunctional," and that says it well. Listen to the moods and messages fighting it out in his head.

Vince wakes up in the morning and his Willpower is in charge (or has the biggest mouth), and after breakfast, he decides not to eat anything until lunch. Hope seconds the motion. But in a few minutes, Make Yourself Happy speaks up and, shouting down Willpower, convinces Vince to give up and get himself a treat. So one moment he's all set to follow his plan; the next moment he's staring into the refrigerator.

And Vince is surprised—just a minute ago, he had decided to stop snacking and the decision seemed so 100 percent trustworthy. And now it's all gone, gone down the drain, nothing left of it, and he's perfectly willing to overeat again. Then Guilt speaks up and tortures him, and he's stressed and challenged, and the next moment, he hears the voice of Failure.

This is what I call an out-of-control committee meeting, and it can tie you up for a few minutes, or it can ruin your whole day.

Thus, in the middle of the afternoon, Vince feels back in control of his eating. But by dinnertime, he's doubting himself, and after dinner, he's frustrated and a little afraid. That evening, his What's the Matter with Me? committee member takes the floor and tries to revive his Willpower. But by bedtime, he's so stuck in committee, tired and depressed, that the I'll Always Be Fat member just feels like stuffing himself with food to shut everybody up and feel better.

Be assured that, whatever your challenge might be, this sort of thing will go on and on. The mind in turmoil is restless, always changing, voice on top of voice. It's an out-of-control committee meeting of all sides of you. And the bad news is that, like Vince, most people get stuck in committee, seemingly at the mercy of this babble of inner voices, tossed back and forth, bounced from thought to thought, from feeling to feeling.

But the good news is that with more awareness, acceptance, and expression, you can start to restore order and get yourself out of committee.

The Committee Meeting

When you're caught up in mind chatter like this, take a few moments to prepare for an orderly Find Your Voice Committee Meeting. Some writing is involved, and (as before) I want you to do it with your non-dominant hand. This will connect you to your voice, your intuition, your TruSage.

The first thing is just to be aware. So with your journal (or just a pad of paper) and pencil in hand, close your eyes, maybe notice your breathing, and just focus on your challenge. This has been a big issue in your life probably for a long time—you've likely had some success and some failure in dealing with it. Well, now you're going to start by just being aware of everything you think and feel about it . . .

Just keep focusing on your issue, your challenge—let your thoughts and feelings flow—and when you're ready, write down on the pad or in your journal what you think and feel about this issue, with your eyes closed, and preferably with your non-dominant hand. It's fine if it looks like scribbling, doodling, or childlike writing. It's not going to be read by anyone else. Write down all the different thoughts and feelings you have about your issue. For example, are you doubtful? Are you judgmental? Do you feel frustrated? Do you feel hopeless, guilty, afraid, angry, or sad? Make a list of all your thoughts and feelings. If nothing comes at first, stay with it for a minute or two; try asking yourself, "What part of me is talking? Whose voice is this?"

Let's say your list includes Afraid, Hopeful, Why Me? Who I Should Be, Frustrated, Guilty, and Angry. These are your seven committee members, your seven different thoughts and feelings about your issue. Just becoming aware of them has already helped you face your challenge. But this time we're going further and adding in the magic of acceptance.

So, with your pad and pencil, or in your journal, and maybe going back and forth between your dominant and non-dominant hands, draw seven circles arranged like chairs around a large round conference table. Now, to give your committee members their proper seat at the table, write one of their names in each of the seven circles. Beautiful. Finally, in the upper right-hand corner of the paper, draw a large heart and write in it the word "Observer." This is your true, authentic self, who acts as the committee chairperson, and who recognizes and accepts all your thoughts and feelings.

Have your Observer look at each circle, at each committee member, at each thought or feeling, one at a time, with friendliness, caring, and compassion. As your Observer looks at each committee member, one after the other, you're learning how to accept all your thoughts and feelings, and thus how to accept yourself just as you are.

Soon we're going deeper into this Find Your Voice visualization. But first let me remind you that if the feelings in this exercise get to be too much, too stressful, or if you just need a break at any time during your Committee Meeting, you can always take a deep breath and get yourself back to the Observer's seat in the corner of the room. From there, you can look on more calmly and with more compassion.

So get yourself comfortable. Breathe deeply and focus on your turning points. Imagine yourself walking down a flight of carpeted stairs to the committee room . . . and then over to the conference table. It's a big circular table, of highly polished wood, and there are different committee members sitting around the table. Each one of the committee members represents a different part of you, a different feeling, thought, or attitude, or maybe a different age or stage in your life. And maybe you already know the name of the first committee member. If you need to look at your list, you can.

So whenever you're ready, take your seat in the corner of the room and let this healing and freeing process begin. You know the issue, the challenge—you know what you're working on. And with your non-dominant hand and just allowing it to move across the paper, give the first committee member a chance to speak. Let the first committee member, whether it's Angry or Afraid or Guilty— whoever it is—have the time to express its thoughts and feelings, from your heart to your head to your hand. Maybe there's Anger at yourself for having this trouble, or at others for giving it to you.

Maybe there's Fear of failing again, or of succeeding this time. Maybe you're Guilty that you feel certain desires, or that you have hateful thoughts. No matter what it is, allow the thoughts and feelings to flow. Write down exactly what this committee member thinks and feels about your issue.

Doodling, drawing, scribbling, words, pictures. You're allowing this part of you to express itself at last. Finally, this committee member can say whatever it wants to about your issue. Let yourself be completely and unconditionally accepting of this part of you, as though it's a child who really needs to be listened to, who needs to get it all out. No more pushing down, no more repressing, no more holding back. Accepting and expressing. Accepting and letting go. From your heart to your head to your hand.

When you're ready, when you feel you've heard everything that this first committee member thinks and feels, go to the next committee member and listen to what it has to say about your issue. Go at your own pace. There's no rush. There's no race. If you need to peek at the name of the next committee member, that's fine. If you can tell who needs to speak next, that's fine too. Just let go, let go. Accepting everything this second committee member thinks and feels and expresses about your issue, without judging, without criticism, without holding back. Just accepting and expressing. Accepting and letting go.

And then go to the next committee member. Continue with your own evolution until you get all the way around your whole committee, one at a time. In Vince's case, maybe there was a ten-year-old ("I really want a hamburger, fries, and a Coke"), or a fifteen-year-old ("I hate myself—I look so fat"), or a twenty-year-old ("Nobody's going to hire a fat person"). Maybe there's an adult

Vince ("I've got to start getting in shape") or a parental Vince ("You need to take responsibility for your weight"). Go ahead and accept each committee member, one at a time. Go all the way around the table; express all the feelings, all the thoughts, all the pictures, all the words.

Finally, you have this opportunity. It may even feel like you've been waiting for years and years. You have the opportunity right here, right now, to give each committee member a voice, to be accepted, expressed, and released. And as you accept and express, accept and let go, you'll discover immediately and forever how much lighter you feel, how much freer you feel, how much better you feel about how you're taking care of yourself from this day forward.

The Committee Meeting is so important in the Find Your Voice process because it gives you an effective, organized way to manage your whole collection of committee members. You can't fire them, you know. You can manage your committee members, and they can get smaller, quieter, and feel more a part of the team, but there isn't any technique anywhere that will let you eliminate them. You could spend your whole life in therapy, you could read all the books, attend all the seminars, you could take all the medication in the world, you could do anything and everything and you're not going to get rid of your committee members.

In a word, you're "stuck" with your committee members. But you don't have to be stuck *in committee* with them. If you become aware of your feelings, accept them, and express them—give them an honest voice and a proper hearing—you'll feel better and freer within a few minutes.

It's the same with your thoughts. You'll always think and you'll always have some negative, critical thoughts. You can't stop yourself from thinking negatively at times, and if you try, you only become more negative and self-critical. But when you recognize your negative thoughts, accept them, and express them to yourself, you feel relaxed and peaceful in no time at all.

It's just that simple. You can manage your feelings and thoughts (your committee members), or they can manage you. If you want to make positive changes in your life, you really have no choice. You have to acknowledge your thoughts and feelings, you have to accept them, and you have to express them. And holding a Committee Meeting is a great way to accomplish this.

Use The Committee Meeting technique as often as you like, on any issue that's troubling you. It's the Find Your Voice process at its best.

Yin and Yang

There's a compelling reason why you can't just simply get rid of those troublesome thoughts and feelings you don't like and wish would go away. It's the principle of yin and yang, that is, the idea in ancient Chinese philosophy that the things of the world, including your thoughts and feelings, are always intertwined with their opposites. (By the way, this is the principle elegantly and delightfully at play in the Chinese finger puzzle, the toy where freedom and entrapment are bound together in a little braided tube.)

This means that as you try to cope with your challenge, you're better off understanding and accepting that you'll always feel both positives and negatives—hopeful and hopeless, kindly and critical, courageous and afraid, and so on—each balanced exquisitely with its opposite.

The following is a meditation on the deeper truth of yin and yang. Read it slowly and softly, and you will hear your wise, healing inner voice.

> Look at a river flowing in its banks.
> You might think the two banks are separate or opposite
> things.
> But look deeper and you see that the two banks aren't
> separate at all.
> They're joined together underneath, at the river bottom.
> And the two banks, joined in the deep bed below, allow
> the river to flow.
> But the conscious mind cannot think so deeply.
> It thinks on surfaces, and so it thinks in extremes: this or
> that, positive or negative, good or bad.
> But the truth is, you're working against yourself if you
> choose sides.
> Be aware and accept that the two banks are both part
> of the river.
> And the river flows swiftly because both banks hold
> strong.
>
> People working on their challenges have told me,
> shaking their heads:
> "Yesterday I was in control, and today I have almost
> none."

Well, control never happens by itself; loss of control is
bound to follow.
Watch the waves at the beach; they do the same thing.
A really big set of waves is followed by a long lull.
So one minute you're the big waves, the next minute
you're the lull.
One day your control is strong, the next day it's weak.
Where there are peaks, there are valleys.
Be aware and accepting of both.
Enjoy the control while it lasts, and enjoy the loss of
control when it comes.
Control is exciting, but nobody can stay excited all the
time.
And what's wrong with letting go and losing control
once in a while? It can be relaxing. And fun.

Breathing, too, is not all inhales or exhales, not "either …
or."
It's the union of the two that creates the flow of breath.
The breath comes in and the breath goes out—you have
a rhythm, and it's the rhythm that keeps you alive.
Trust your rhythm and enjoy both your inhales and your
exhales.
It's no good choosing one side or the other.
Life is in the balance.

Open and Close

The idea of life as a dynamic balance of opposites (or dialectic) is one of those truly profound insights that reaches across cultural boundaries and transcends time. It's part not only of ancient Taoist thinking but also of Greek, Hindu, Buddhist, Talmudic, and nineteenth-century German philosophy. And it shows up again in some simple, elegant lines by Jalal ad-Din Rumi, a thirteenth-century Sufi scholar, mystic, and poet of self-discovery:

> Your hand opens and closes and opens and closes.
> If it were always a fist or always stretched open,
> you would be paralyzed.
> Your deepest presence is in every small contracting
> and expanding,
> the two as beautifully balanced and coordinated
> as bird wings.

The next time you find yourself under stress, trying with all your might to get rid of your negative feelings, just open and close your hand a few times. Maybe even practice this in your daily life for a while. Open and close . . . open and close. This will help you feel the rhythm of life as a synergy and maybe encourage you to acknowledge and accept both sides of yourself.

Not Perfect, but Perfectly Okay

Like Diane with her "should's," most people struggling with personal challenges have lost this sense of balance and live with an expectation of perfection. They believe it's all about "fixing" themselves for good or finally "getting rid" of what's wrong with them. Then when they make mistakes, which, of course, happens every day—many times a day—they reject themselves, judge themselves, and beat themselves up with self-criticism. They feel they've failed themselves. Was I too weak? Was I too lazy? Am I a bad person? Why can't I do this? And so their challenge goes on and on.

These people's real mistake—and it guaranteed they would fall short of their goals—was in not allowing themselves to make mistakes, was in not embracing themselves, not enjoying themselves, mistakes and all.

As you finish with Step 1, it's really important to understand that, no matter how conscientiously you practice or how well you master these Find Your Voice techniques, you're not going to achieve perfection. Fully experiencing your challenge doesn't mean that the challenge miraculously vanishes. You'll still have your share of fears, angers, pains, cravings, and the like; it's just that with more awareness, acceptance, and expression, you'll be better able to handle them and minimize their role in your life.

In short, you won't be perfect but perfectly okay.

The Guest House

Near the end of our work together, when she was feeling much more relaxed, Diane told me her secret: "I've learned to make friends with both my demons and my angels. I've started to recognize and laugh at the 'should's' in my life, and consequently life has been lighter."

Life has been lighter. This is exactly what happens when you begin to become aware of, to accept, and to express all sides of yourself—all your "should's" and "shouldn'ts," positives and negatives, goods and bads. Life is filled with all these competing thoughts and feelings—you can't get away from them—and your best self-care lies in learning the life lesson they teach: Don't fight them, don't try to control them, but experience them with joy and embrace them all as they come.

And the rich irony is that, when you can finally come to laugh a little at your own imperfection, you discover in your laughter the powerful voice of your deep inner wisdom.

Rumi sums this up brilliantly in another simple poem of timeless insight into what it means to experience yourself as a whole human being.

THE GUEST HOUSE

This being human is a guest house.
Every morning a new arrival.

A joy, a depression, a meanness,
some momentary awareness comes
as an unexpected visitor.

Welcome and entertain them all!
Even if they're a crowd of sorrows,
who violently sweep your house
empty of its furniture,
still, treat each guest honorably.
He may be clearing you out
for some new delight.
The dark thought, the shame, the malice,
meet them at the door laughing,
and invite them in.

Be grateful for whoever comes,
because each has been sent
as a guide from beyond.

CHAPTER 2

Judge Your Challenge

J eff called himself a pornography "addict." He hated the "secret life" of his obsession with porn, and he hated himself because he couldn't stop sneaking a look at hard core sex. He felt he was always tailing himself, and he said in disgust, "I'm not the kind of person I want to be."

Kris was quick to put herself down, calling herself "uptight," a "control freak," and "ready for nothing." She compared herself to her sister, who was just the opposite, "relaxed, two kids, a nice person, etc." Kris chain-smoked, and she blamed herself for not being able to quit her habit.

Rick couldn't control his fears—of conflict, of rejection, of dying—and he came down hard on himself for being so weak. It seemed "ridiculous" to him that someone as smart as he was couldn't figure it out. He knew he was "his own biggest critic," but he felt he didn't deserve to be happy.

Sandy was full of "guilt and regrets" from a failed marriage. She also had bouts of deep sadness and hopelessness, and she couldn't stand feeling that way. She hated crying and feeling helpless, feeling "I can't fix it." So she tried to drink her problems away, but her stomach couldn't take it.

From my work with thousands of clients like Jeff, Kris, Rick, and Sandy, I've come to the conclusion that people struggling with personal issues and challenges carry within themselves a crushing load of self-criticism. It's as if they have a severe, relentless judge inside of them whose job is to criticize, to condemn, and to punish them for their less-than-perfect thoughts, feelings, and behavior. This is the Inner Judge I described in the Introduction; it's the Inner Critic who sits in the fifteenth row and views your life movie only to find fault with it. This is the blaming, complaining, over-analyzing, never-satisfied, know-it-all, controlling, comparing, greedy, demanding, worried, always-please-others, "I'm not good enough," "What do they think of me?" "This isn't going to work" part of you, and it can be a loud, negative voice in your head that runs continually, day and night.

Can You Break Free?

I'm certainly not the first to recognize this judgmental portion of our nature. In 1923 Freud famously named it the "superego," and then Thomas Harris in *I'm OK, You're OK* (1967)—the first modern blockbuster self-help book—called it our inner "parent." More recently, Don Miguel Ruiz in *The Four*

Agreements (1997) speaks about the "Big Judge and Book of Laws" inside of us, and Eckhart Tolle in his bestsellers *The Power of Now* (1999) and *A New Earth* (2005) calls it the "ego" or the "egoic mind."

However, even though I admire Ruiz's and Tolle's work, and agree with much of what they have to say about the origin and nature of the Judge/ego, I very respectfully disagree with them about what we need *to do* with it. Ruiz and Tolle both believe you must try to get rid of this part of yourself. Ruiz says you must become a "Warrior" and fight to "free yourself of the tyranny of the Judge." Tolle takes a gentler view, but says virtually the same thing: By learning "the wisdom of non-judgment," you can "break free" from your critical mind and bring about "the end of the ego."

But my thirty years of practical experience counseling thousands of clients tells me there's no breaking free from your Inner Judge/Critic/ego. There's no getting rid of it. There's no therapy or medication or level of enlightenment that will eliminate it. People try all the time—some try all their lives—to fight and conquer this part of themselves, but it just doesn't go away.

The Guru with a Toothache

To show you what I mean, let me tell you a true story.

I went to India in 1997 to teach mind-body healing, but I also went to learn from the famous gurus who lived and worked there. In my studies, I had read about a state of "enlightenment" that some of these gurus had attained, and I wanted to see who had gotten there and how they had accomplished this marvelous feat. I thought if it was possible to become fully enlightened like this, I wanted to be let in on the secret.

I met many wonderful teachers on my tour, but on one of my stops I stayed with a truly amazing guru: brilliant, simple, powerful, calming, peaceful, strong, humble, and totally present. Because of my own status as a teacher, I got to visit "backstage" and was privileged to see parts of his private life— his bedroom, bathroom, library, and so forth—that nobody else sees.

One morning before I was going to make my presentation to the members of his ashram (he was going to introduce me), we were sitting in his beautiful library *filled* with books on philosophy, spirituality, healing, transcendence, meditation, and the like. He was not talking, though that didn't seem surprising for he was a man of few words.

But this was different. I noticed he was holding his mouth, and then he let out a sound that was in between an "Om" humming and a call for help.

I asked if I could do anything. He said, "Probably not," and he briefly explained that he had a bad toothache and was waiting for his dentist to arrive. Two of my books have chapters on healing, relaxation, pain control, and specific techniques for dental work, so I mentioned these (and he had my books in his library), but he said, "No thanks." He'd wait for his dentist.

The dentist phoned and must have said he was running a little late, because the guru told him, "My tooth hurts and I'm about to make a presentation to the ashram. Can you hurry up?" The dentist must have said he was already hurrying because the guru said, "Can you hurry faster?"

The tension was building, probably like the toothache.

The guru was in pain, aggravated, and showing that he was not happy at all. He told me that this dentist "always has an excuse" but that he was his favorite dentist because he used nitrous gas, went to a very good American dental school, and was always on time, adding crossly, "Well, not this time." Then he made a few more irritable comments about the dentist being late.

After thirty or so very awkward minutes, the dentist arrived and soon completed his treatment. In no time at all, the guru was comfortable and happy again, and ready to meet with his followers.

The scene was fascinating to watch, and most instructive. Waiting for the dentist, the guru's serene enlightenment vanished, and for a while he was as human—impatient, complaining, critical—as any of the rest of us. Then when his toothache was gone, he relaxed and his enlightenment quickly returned.

So I did indeed learn a valuable lesson, although it was not the one that I had expected. I learned that "enlightenment" is not a permanent, constant state of mind you attain once and for all, but a spiritual process you must practice every day. And I also learned that even the most enlightened persons—masters of inner peace—still carry their Inner Judge within them.

A Lifetime Membership

So again, in my view, the Inner Judge is an integral, ineradicable part of you—it has a lifetime membership. It's the sum total of all your childhood conditioning to be critical, mistrustful, and self-doubting. It's the negativity implanted by all the people—parents, siblings, teachers, coaches, "friends" and enemies—who've ever punished you or bullied you. It's the egotism and vanity ("it's all about me") taught by much of popular culture—by high fashion and Hollywood stars, by TV, rock music, and sports celebrities. It even includes your own judgmental personality traits. No matter how hard you try, you can't just throw away all of this programming and replace it with something new. In the home theater of your mind, you can't just choose a different movie if you don't like the one you're starring in.

And why should you try to get rid of your Inner Judge? To me, the Inner Judge is a *quality*—a part of your nature that can help you in life, when, for instance, you need to make smart decisions, to stick up for yourself, to deal with numbers or schedules, to drive your car, and so forth. In contrast (and this really sets us apart), both Ruiz and Tolle call the Inner Judge a psychic "parasite" that keeps you in misery so it can feed on your pain.

Thus, to me, the problem is not that you *have* an Inner Judge; the problem is how you *handle* it. When you try to fight your Inner Judge, when you try to silence it, defeat it, replace it, reprogram it, dominate it, you actually accomplish just the opposite: You give it so much energy that it grows strong and comes to dominate you.

Here again is the trap I described in Step 1: The harder you work to "break free" of your Inner Judge, the more judgmental you become—you are, in effect, *judging* your Judge—and this only locks in your challenge.

What You Resist Will Persist

So, what can you do with your Inner Judge? The answer brings us to the vital second step in the Find Your Voice process.

The answer is, after you fully experience your challenge, you need to take a few minutes and *let yourself judge yourself.* That's right. Go ahead and let your Inner Judge have its say. Let your Inner Critic stand up in the fifteenth row and speak its mind. In this way, you give your Inner Judge the same attention and respect you gave your challenge itself in Step 1, that is, you become *aware* of it, you *accept* it, and you *express* it. Only by acknowledging your Inner Judge, recognizing it, allowing it, listening to it, working with it—making it part of the team—can you make peace with this negative part of yourself and quiet its voice.

It might seem paradoxical, but this is how human nature works. What you resist will persist, and will fight you every step of the way, but what you become aware of, accept, and express will stop fighting back, will relax, and will diminish in a matter of minutes.

And here's the most important point: Only by healing the relationship with your fifteenth-row Critic and softening its voice can you hope to move to the last row and hear the voice of your inner wisdom.

Tied Up in "Not's"

The first task, then, is to become aware of your Inner Judge. But this is easier said than done. In most cases, your Inner Judge is so familiar to you, so much a part of you, so thoroughly programmed in your brain, that you don't even know it's there.

In my observation, 95 percent of people dealing with physical or emotional challenges live 95 percent of their lives in an inner atmosphere of self-criticism, condemnation, and judgment. They continually say things to themselves that simply aren't true—that they are *not* good enough, *cannot* help themselves, and will *not* succeed, also that they are *not* as good a person as they should be, and do *not* deserve to be happy. This negative self-talk goes on and on like a broken record. This is what I call being "tied up in 'not's,'" and it's second nature for so many of the people I work with.

Now, the voice of the Inner Judge isn't just mildly annoying background noise; it's always an essential part of your challenge, always deeply involved in intensifying and prolonging your anxiety, craving, pain, anger, sadness, and so forth. You know how it goes. You work hard trying to fix yourself, to feel better, but you don't get anywhere. You argue, debate with yourself for hours, and think you've solved one problem—and five more pop up. Why? Because your Inner Judge is contrary in nature and is never satisfied with you or your solutions. It takes its job very, *very* seriously, and so sends you message after message (it hardly ever shuts up) of self-doubt, unhappiness, disapproval, failure, suspicion, on and on.

So, when it comes to managing your challenge, you simply won't make much progress unless you first learn how to manage your Inner Judge and keep it from dominating your life. Not get rid of it, mind you, but just let it loosen up and relax. Let it rest for a little while. I call this getting yourself unstuck from the fifteenth row, and the process starts with recognizing that you've been living with your Inner Judge since you were a child.

The Parent Trap

The origin of self-judgment is almost always in childhood, specifically in your parents' judgments and criticisms as they try to control you and make you behave.

For example, my client, Vince (whom I mentioned in Step 1), was taught as a boy at home to be critical of himself. Whenever he tried to share his sadness and frustration about being the "fat kid" in school, his parents would stop him and tell him, "Pull yourself together," "Don't be a crybaby," "You should forget about it." He quickly learned that the only way to please his parents was to come down hard on himself—to judge himself as quickly and severely as they did.

This judgmental, critical attitude took its toll on the whole family. Both of Vince's parents, his brother, and his two sisters were also seriously overweight, nearly obese. If feelings were criticized and stifled in the family, food was always a big deal, and the more food the better. Food, you see, was the family's coping mechanism; overeating was how they all dealt with their feelings. Unable to accept or express themselves emotionally, they were stuffing their feelings down with food.

Another client, Mary, told me, "I know when I'm trying to cope with the demands of my three small kids, I will lose my patience at some point. I'm not aware of the process of how I get to that point or when it will arrive. Sometimes, I'll yell at the kids . . . and then I feel so ashamed." Here's an Inner Judge in fine form: Mary is critical of her kids *and* critical of herself for being critical.

As I've said before, I'm not blaming Vince's parents, or Mary, or any other parents in particular. Most parents are trapped in the fifteenth row themselves, dealing with their own Inner Critic. They're doing the best they can, and they're just passing on issues that were given to them by their own parents. But the fact remains: Your Inner Judge is born in childhood and grows strong in a critical family atmosphere.

This happens in some degree to almost all of us. Most parents are well-meaning but know nothing better than to try to make their kids mind them by spanking them, yelling at them, scolding them, penalizing them. And so they give their kids daily lessons in how to be—and that it's *right* to be—judgmental and punishing.

But beyond that, most children are extremely sensitive to conflict in the family and tend to blame themselves for any tensions, for any strained relations, for any lack of love—or far worse problems—and they can easily begin to feel "It's my fault," or "Something must be wrong with me," or "I must have done something wrong." Because these false statements are so highly charged with emotion, they can, if repeated often enough, turn into self-defining negative judgments that last a lifetime.

In this way, and all too often, parents program their kids for unhappiness.

Family Origins

It's time now to become more aware of your own negative programming; it's time to begin recognizing your Inner Judge by getting in touch with the family relationships that gave rise to it.

The following short quiz will help you get started. For each question, circle the "a" or "b" response. Take your time, give each question some thought, and be as honest as you can be. Don't worry for now about shielding you parents—for personal growth, honesty is always the best policy.

THE FAMILY ORIGINS QUIZ

1. My memories of my mother are
   a. distressing and unhappy much of the time
   b. peaceful and happy much of the time

2. My parents' relationship was often
   a. angry and strained
   b. loving and mutually respectful

3. When I think of my father, I mostly feel
   a. a sense of distance and coolness
   b. a sense of closeness and warmth

4. My mother showed me affection
   a. with difficulty and only occasionally
   b. naturally and quite often

5. In my family, I
   a. felt I had to hide my feelings
   b. felt free to share my feelings

6. My father played with me
   a. rarely and with difficulty
   b. regularly and easily

7. Overall, I feel my parents were
   a. disappointed in me
   b. proud of me

8. When I made mistakes, I often
   a. felt criticized and punished
   b. felt loved and supported

9. My parents expected me to be
   a. obedient
   b. independent

10. My mother was more
    a. cautious and protective
    b. brave and encouraging

11. My parents wanted me to be more
    a. humble
    b. self-confident

12. My father was more
    a. careful and controlling
    b. easy-going and tolerant

SCORING

The number of your "a" responses is a good indicator of how deeply your Inner Judge was implanted in your childhood, and thus how much it dominates you now as an adult. Count up your "a" responses, and locate yourself on the following Inner Judge scale.

1–3 "A" RESPONSES: MILDLY CRITICAL

You often feel inadequate and a little guilty, as if you're not good enough, or that you must have done something wrong. Little things upset you and you can get frustrated and nervous. You feel critical of others, but you also try very hard to please others. You want to do things just right, but you're never satisfied with the results.

4–6 "A" RESPONSES: HIGHLY CRITICAL

You feel inferior and ashamed of yourself, and you beat yourself up for your smallest mistakes. Often tense and angry, you wish you were better than you are, and you feel driven to fix yourself. You're judgmental and quick to criticize others, and yet you need the approval of others. You even try to impress others and hate yourself for being so false.

7 OR MORE "A" RESPONSES: SEVERELY CRITICAL

You feel worthless and deeply flawed, and you believe you don't deserve to be happy. You feel taken over by "bad" thoughts, feelings, and habits, and you try to control yourself and fight off your demons. You're critical of others, but even more critical of yourself. You feel you have to be perfect, but you know you can never measure up.

Looking Back

If the Family Origins Quiz has gotten you started looking back at the role your parents (or parental figures) played in implanting your own Inner Judge, it's a good idea to follow up while the memories and feelings are fresh. Here's an introspective Find Your Voice exercise that will help you dig down into the roots of the problem.

Before you begin, find a few minutes to be quiet and alone. Sit in a comfortable chair, take several deep, satisfying breaths, and have your journal and pencil close at hand.

Now, with your eyes closed, let your mind wander over your childhood and try to remember times in your family when you felt criticized harshly or were punished severely. Listen for your true, authentic voice as you delve into your feelings. Did you feel fear, resentment, guilt, anger, sadness? When the memories start to come, go ahead and jot them down in your journal (using your non-dominant hand, even scribbling, doodling, or drawing). You can open your eyes to get started on the page, but then write blind.

You might ask yourself: Is there some person or people responsible for your feeling criticized, judged, or punished? Was it your mother? Your father? Both parents? Some other parental figure or figures?

Try to recall in detail what was happening at the time. Were you harshly criticized or punished at home? Inside or outside? If inside, in what room? What time of day? Was the punishment violent (spanking or whipping or worse)? Was it verbal (blaming or scolding or worse)? Can you associate a face with this experience? A facial expression? Can you put a voice to this experience? A tone of voice? Any smells? Any body sensations?

What was the reason you were being severely criticized or punishment? Did you break a family rule? Did you talk back? Did you show anger? Weakness? Was it about your choice of friends? Your grades? Your style of dress or hair? Your manners? Your attitude?

What was the family dynamic at the time? Were both of your parents upset with you? Or were they fighting over you, one parent criticizing you and the other taking your part? Did you feel responsible for their arguing? Did you feel it was your fault?

You'll probably need to visit these memories a number of times before you become fully aware of your childhood experiences. You might even find some resistance to uncovering the details. Be patient and open, and allow the scenes to emerge as they will.

The "Boogeyman" in the Closet

To illustrate how powerful this memory work can be, consider the case of Rick, whom I mentioned at the start of this chapter.

Rick had been suffering from mild anxiety attacks all his life, but now as he was getting older, they were getting worse—almost full-scale panic attacks—and he didn't know what to do anymore. I began introducing him to the Find Your Voice process, and as we got started, Rick took a long look at his childhood. What he found was most revealing.

Rick remembered that by the age of ten he was already showing signs of having a problem with anxiety. He had wet the bed for a while, he had stuttered at times, he had bouts of insomnia, he was deathly afraid of the dark and of the "boogeyman" in the closet, and he had already developed a small stomach ulcer. Now he asked himself: How had so much tension and fear seeped into such a young boy?

As Rick started to let his memories unfold, it became clear to him that his parents were both dominated by their Inner Judge. His mother was fiercely overprotective and immaculately clean, and his dad was a serious workaholic and a strict disciplinarian—a "spare the rod, spoil the child" sort of man. Rick's mother scolded him for the slightest things: for getting his jeans grass-stained playing, for tracking dirt into the house, for getting mad and fighting with his older brother, for neglecting his household chores or schoolwork.

When he was especially "bad" (that is, defiant or sassing), his father would whip him, sometimes with a belt. Rick remembered his mother once telling him, "You're going to get the belt when your father gets home from work," and Rick had to wait in terror for hours, checking at the front window, or listening for the sound of his dad's car pulling into the driveway.

With all this, Rick came to believe that he was bad and deserved to be punished. He felt he was always at fault and was even to blame for his parents fighting. One night when he was about twelve, he heard his parents arguing loudly in the kitchen, and then he heard his father stomp out, slam the door, and drive off in the car. Rick thought they must be fighting about him, and he was in agony, sobbing in his bedroom, feeling that he had made his father leave. Even when his dad returned half an hour later, Rick couldn't help feeling that maybe he was causing his parents to split up.

The grown-up Rick wanted to be fair to his parents, and he reminded himself that there was a good deal of love and a good sense of humor in the family—a surprising amount considering what his parents had gone through in their own lives. Both had been raised in the Depression. His mother's first marriage had quickly ended in divorce, and his father had fought in World War II. Also, his mom's father had died when she was a little girl, and his dad's mother, an alcoholic, had abandoned him when he was just a boy.

So Rick's parents certainly had huge issues of their own, and no doubt they had done a remarkable job overcoming them and making a family. But now, hearing his voice, Rick also realized that both his parents lived with a dominant Inner Judge, and for the first time he knew that they had passed this critical, anxious, fearful, blaming, punishing mindset onto him.

Family Legacy

This, then, is the legacy of a Judge-driven family. Once you've learned in childhood (for whatever reasons) to judge yourself harshly—once you're convinced that there's something wrong with you and you need to be punished—you exercise this judging muscle every day, and it grows into a fully developed, domineering adult Inner Judge. You give this Inner Critic a reserved seat in the fifteenth row, and it eagerly goes to work finding fault with you and everybody else involved in the movie of your life.

Just think of how often in your day you're busy criticizing yourself, evaluating yourself, comparing yourself, judging yourself and others. How often you're critical of your appearance, your performance, your achievements, of your spouse, your kids, your neighbors, of drivers on the road, politicians, celebrities—the list goes on and on.

More importantly, think how often in your day you're critical of yourself and your life in regard to your challenge. How often you're critical of your thoughts, your feelings, your habits, your weaknesses, your flaws, your failures, even of your successes.

When you start keeping track, you'll soon realize that your Inner Judge is relentless, tireless, and ruthless. It might surprise you. In no time at all, you'll see that your Inner Judge is nuts. Completely bonkers. An ego maniac. A control freak. Selfish. Up-tight. Never satisfied, perfectionist, possessive. Feels inferior, inadequate, defensive, and so much more.

And that's okay. No one is perfect. No one will ever be perfect. As I've said before, you'll never get rid of your Inner Judge. Its internal monologue will go on and on. But you can learn how to keep its voice from dominating you and locking you into your challenge. You can learn how to turn the volume down and, for a little while, get yourself unstuck from the fifteenth row.

Four Degrees of Awareness

Just becoming aware that you *have* an Inner Judge—and that you've had it from childhood—will help you quiet its voice a good deal. It likes the attention. But even more helpful is learning to observe yourself with finer and finer degrees of awareness.

Most times you become aware of your Inner Judge only *after* you've been critical of yourself or others, only later on, when the crisis has passed, when the heat of the moment has cooled and you've "come back" to yourself. Thus, Mary becomes aware of her sudden harshness a few minutes after she's yelled at her kids, when it's too late and the damage has been done. By the way, this is when you're most liable to pile on the self-criticism, to become critical of yourself for being so critical. In Mary's case, she becomes ashamed of herself for being angry.

However, it's also possible to become aware of your Inner Judge *during* the critical act itself, while it's happening. For Mary, it's right during her explosion at her kids, or in the midst of her shame. *See if you can sense it: The criticism is there like smoke inside you. Becoming aware in the very thick of it—that's the challenge. At first, maybe you become aware of it after one minute. The next time you become aware just as your negativity is evaporating, just when the smoke is clearing. Then comes a moment when you become aware exactly in the middle of it.*

The next and even finer challenge is to become aware of your Inner Judge before the act, when the critical judgment is just arising inside you. *Try to catch hold of it: It's there like a seed, ready to spring to life at any moment, but right now it's still only a niggling feeling in the back of your mind.* For Mary, it's still only a vague feeling of impatience and helplessness when trying to cope with her kids. Recognizing your Inner Judge's negative energy in this early stage, before it swells into critical action, might seem impossible to you right now. But it can be done.

So, when dealing with your Inner Judge there are always three degrees of awareness: before, during, and after. And yet there's also a fourth degree—really another level of awareness—that can, with practice, help you manage your Inner Judge expertly. This fourth degree is *higher* awareness, when you're able to take a step back, go to the last row, become aware of the other three degrees of awareness—wherever you are with your Inner Judge—and say to yourself in your wise, healing inner voice: *"I know I'm getting upset. I'll watch myself. I'll be more aware, I'll breathe, notice my tension, listen to my thoughts and feelings, and maybe, with more awareness, I can, this time, let my Inner Judge have a rest."*

The Racehorse

To develop a healthier, more cooperative relationship with your Inner Judge, you need to keep refining your awareness, but you also need to add in the power of acceptance and expression. The following Find Your Voice technique is a good way to begin.

The next time you feel caught up in your challenge, go to your bedroom, or private place, close the door, and for ten minutes listen to your Inner Judge talking inside your head, just as you would listen to any person talking. But for now remain separate, detached, uninvolved. Just listen to what that one part of your mind is saying. Whatever comes, let it come. Allow it. Don't try to ignore it or repress it. Only observe and listen.

Awareness is not an action, you know, nothing you have to do. No effort, nothing special; just sitting quietly, here, now, in the present, you will be aware. In Zen meditation, this is called "Sati," which means "mindfulness" or "right awareness." The English Romantic poet William Wordsworth called it a "wise passiveness."

You'll probably notice right away that a lot of trash talk has gathered over the years, and it will come out now all in a rush. When given this freedom, the Inner Judge will run like a racehorse that has broken out of its corral. "I'm going nowhere in my life," "I just can't do this," "Every time I try to change, I fail," "I just don't like me," "Why should I try if it's not going to work anyway," "I'm no good," "I'll always be weak," "Just this once won't hurt," "I can't help myself," "I don't know what's wrong with me," "I've tried, but I just can't."

Let your mind run! Let the negative self-talk flow! Let it go! You simply sit, accept, and listen. This is the art of patience.

Now, you'll find that you want badly to catch this runaway horse, bridle it, control it, direct it this way and that. This is your social/family programming, your old habit of repression. Your Inner Judge is actually afraid of the freedom you've given it and will almost immediately judge what's happening—"Why are you thinking all this? Be careful!"—and try to have you get back on the horse and rein it in. You'll have to be patient and persistent in order to keep detached, hands off, merely observing and listening.

As your Inner Judge races around, go ahead and express all your thoughts and feelings. Speak them out loud, or to yourself, or jot them down in your journal (using your non-dominant hand, and so doodling and scribbling are just as likely as words). These thoughts and feelings can be loud or subtle; some might shout at you and some might whisper. Just remain totally unbiased and neutral, well-detached from them, and speak or write out whatever comes to you. If ranting comes—rant. If abuse comes—abuse. If gossip comes—gossip. (The Inner Judge is filled with gossip!)

Again, this won't be easy. The habit of repression is so strong that you'll forget to stay detached from your Inner Judge. You'll identify yourself with your critical thoughts and feelings, and immediately try to fight them, control them, or get rid of them, as you've always done. You'll try to ride the racehorse once again and direct/correct your thinking and feeling.

But now, with more awareness, you'll feel the failure.

As soon as you notice this urge to control, get back off the horse and let the critical words, thoughts, and feelings run where they will. Just keep observing and listening; keep being aware, accepting, and expressing.

Work with this technique whenever you get the chance. It's absolutely essential for you to express the Inner Judge part of your mind patiently every day, or many times a day if needed, for days, weeks, or even months. You need to convince your Inner Judge that you're willing to listen to it, that you're going to take it into account—that it's part of the team.

If you're sincere and diligent, no matter how long it takes, you'll be able to relax your Inner Judge and tone down its voice. And this will open up some space in your consciousness for your true, authentic voice to be heard.

Interior Monologue

Here's a technique that develops the metaphor of the Inner Critic sitting in the fifteenth row watching the story of your life.

First, imagine you're up on a big movie screen, or on stage at a playhouse, and you're an actor or actress giving a speech, a monologue, a presentation to an almost empty theater—this is all about you—about how things are going in your life right now, about how you're doing with your challenge. You're simply allowing yourself to say what your challenge feels like, acknowledging it, describing it. "The pain is terrible. . . ." "I just can't stop eating. . . ." "It makes me so angry. . . ." "I can't sleep I'm so worried. . . ." "I really need a cigarette. . . ." Let yourself deliver your interior monologue about anything that's troubling you.

Now, move your awareness and become your Inner Critic sitting in the fifteenth row. From the fifteenth-row perspective, watch the actor or actress speaking about your challenge, listen to the monologue, hear all the feelings, all the thoughts. And from the fifteenth-row Inner Critic perspective, focus on what's wrong with the scene—what's wrong with the actor or actress, what's wrong with the thoughts and feelings, what's wrong with being challenged in the first place. The Inner Critic is never satisfied with you or your story, and you'll find it the easiest thing in the world to criticize yourself.

Critics make notes when they're reviewing a movie or play, so using your non-dominant hand, jot down in your journal (scrawl, doodle) all your negative opinions and impressions. "You look awful. . . ." "You're not saying this right. . . ." "Stop whining. . . ." "You should know better. . . ." "You're never going to get well. . . ." "Why do you have to be this way?. . . ." "You've got to stop. . . ."

So clever is your Inner Critic that you might even start criticizing yourself for being critical. "Why are you being so negative? . . ." "You should only think happy thoughts. . . ." "You're only making things worse. . . ."

Let all these self-criticisms spill out for ten minutes, or until you get to one hundred criticisms, which might easily come first.

Interior Dialogue

A powerful Find Your Voice technique is to create an interior dialogue between your personal challenge and your Inner Judge.

On one side is your pain, craving, anxiety, anger, sadness, and so on—all your thoughts and feelings about what you're going through. On the other side is your Inner Judge, emotionally repressing everything, being critical of yourself and everybody else, punishing yourself when you make mistakes.

Now imagine a scene in the movie or the play of your life, a scene of meeting—at a cafe, in a kitchen, or a beautiful garden—anywhere you want. And in this scene a conversation takes place between these two characters, these two sides of you. What would they say to each other? Would they talk to or even recognize each other?

Start with your Inner Judge. What would that side of you say to your challenge? Notice the over-thinking, the moralizing, the self-doubt, the negativity, the impatience, the rigidity. Just say it out loud, think it in your head, or write it down in your journal—whatever works for you.

Then let your personal challenge respond. What would that side of you say? Notice the shallow breathing, the fear, the tension, the mind chatter, the struggle, the shame, the desperation, the vulnerability.

Let the conversation go back and forth for at least ten minutes. Imagine the nonverbal, the verbal, the body language, the facial expressions, the energy that goes back and forth. They're both you, so this dialogue is important. You're not getting rid of either one, so you have to learn how to live with both, how to work with all of you, how to help the two sides coexist.

Finally, move to the fifteenth row and become the Inner Critic watching the scene. (That's right, your Inner Critic will be observing your Inner Judge.) From the fifteenth row, be as critical as you can be of both versions, and of the idea that you can even have these opposing characters inside you at the same time. Scrutinize every aspect of these two versions of you. Let it out, express it all, scribble it (using your non-dominant hand) in your journal.

Critique Your Committee

Okay, let's expand these fifteenth-row techniques even further and get your whole inner committee into the act.

Once again, imagine a scene in the movie or play of your life, only this time you're holding a Committee Meeting about your challenge. Up there on the stage or screen, sitting around the large, highly polished conference table, are the committee members you identified in Step 1. Here are some typical ones: Afraid, Hopeful, Why Me? Who I Should Be, Frustrated, Guilty, and Angry. Remember, your own committee members, whatever your list happens to be, represent your dominant thoughts, feelings, and attitudes about your challenge.

Now, however, instead of just giving each a good listen, I want you to watch the scene from the fifteenth row, sitting in your usual Critic's seat with your journal open and your pencil poised. As the Committee Meeting proceeds, as each committee member gets a chance to speak, go ahead and let your Inner Critic critique each one in turn.

Maybe you feel only wimps or sissies are Afraid; maybe you feel Hopeful is naïve and silly; maybe you think Why Me? is just bellyaching; maybe Who I Should Be is nothing but wishful thinking; maybe being Frustrated is your own fault; maybe feeling Guilty is a punishment you deserve; and maybe getting Angry is just being stupid.

Whatever your criticisms, and no matter how harsh, let your Inner Critic respond to each committee member one at a time, as the camera focuses on them, or as the spotlight finds them. Write down (scribble, doodle, using your non-dominant hand) any judgments that come to mind.

Taking Your Judge for a Walk

Here's a technique that's especially effective because it gets your body involved. Every morning or evening, for days, weeks, or months (and then on an as-needed basis), I want you to take your Inner Judge for a walk.

For ten to thirty minutes, take a walk in your neighborhood, or on a community walking path, or in a park, or at the beach—anywhere you like—and while you're walking, see if you can start to notice your Inner Judge's constant flow of critical opinions.

These might be of the immediate world around you—of your neighbors' houses or yards or cars or kids, or maybe it's too hot or too cold, or too sunny or too cloudy, or maybe there's too much traffic, or too many rocks in the path, or not enough (or too much) sand on the beach.

Then again these criticisms might be of yourself—of your body (too fat, too skinny), of your walking (too fast, too slow), of your breathing (too hard, too shallow), or even of your judgments themselves (too negative, too many). Yes, that's right, when given the chance, your Inner Judge will criticize anything and everything—even itself.

Take at least ten minutes and just be aware of how critical you can be on a walk, by yourself, in a beautiful place, with no one to bother you. Simply listen and watch how your Inner Judge goes on and on. Simply be aware of and accept whatever comes out of your critical mind, and say all these things silently in your head, or softly to yourself.

You aren't trying to stop, control, fix, or get rid of your Inner Judge. You're just taking your Inner Judge for a walk, even though it might seem like it's taking you for a walk, like a big, powerful dog pulling you along by the leash. Who's walking whom? It really doesn't matter because you're learning how to get along with your Inner Judge.

As I've said before, if you try to get rid of your Inner Judge, it will get stronger and more cunning because it will fight for survival. It knows you need it! You always have, always will. It developed in the brain millions of years ago, and has been very useful for thousands of generations. On your walk, for instance, it helps you avoid a busy street, or keep track of how long you've been gone, or remember how to get home.

However, while your Inner Judge needs to be accepted as a necessary part of you, it doesn't have to be involved in everything you do. It's like a chair: very useful when you want to sit down, but you don't need to carry it with you everywhere you go.

So leave your chair at home this time, and after ten to thirty minutes of walking with awareness, acceptance, and expression, find a comfortable spot where you can sit down and relax. Sit on the grass under a tree, or on a park bench, or on the sandy beach, and rest, sweat, breathe deeply, and feel the peace that comes after you've taken your Inner Judge for a walk.

Tired from the exercise, your Inner Judge stops functioning so intensely; it calms down, takes a break, gets smaller and smaller— and your body (which is the seat of your unconscious) has a chance to take over for a few minutes.

First you feel alive in your body, in tune, like your favorite animal, whole, total, free, relaxed. Then gradually your senses sharpen. You begin to notice the cool breeze and hear the rustling of leaves. You see shadows dappling the path. You hear birds singing. In the park, you hear children playing and laughing. At the beach, you feel the warmth of the sand and hear the waves breaking. And finally, very quietly, you begin to hear the sound of silence in your own mind and heart.

These moments of peace and stillness become a meditation in which you hear the true, authentic voice of the world within and without.

The Sorcerer's Apprentice

Becoming aware of, accepting, and expressing your Inner Judge is so vital because for so long, for years or decades, you've been repressing this critical, judgmental part of you. You've been covering it up, trying to stop it, trying to control it, trying to keep yourself and others from knowing what you're like inside. Vince, for instance, was sixty-three years old before he started to acknowledge and express his Inner Judge. Once he did, he started to make rapid progress in losing weight and keeping it off. He's happier and healthier now, and, by the way, he gets along better with his family than ever before.

The problem is, of course—as years of doing this have proven—the harder you try to control your Inner Judge, the more you accomplish just the opposite: the more energy you give it, the more power over your life.

It reminds me of the "The Sorcerer's Apprentice," a ballad originally written in 1797 by the great German poet Goethe, but made popular around the world by Walt Disney in his 1940 animated classic, *Fantasia*.

Remember Disney's version? When a wise old sorcerer leaves his workshop, his apprentice (Mickey Mouse) casts a spell and enchants the broom to fetch water from the well. But the spell is incomplete, and the broom doesn't know when to stop; it tirelessly (almost demonically) carries in and empties bucket after bucket. (All this set to Paul Dukas' marvelous music!)

As the workshop fills with water, Mickey frantically tries—and fails—to control the broom; finally he attacks it with an axe and chops it to pieces. But all his efforts only make matters worse: Each splinter magically arises and grows into a new broom, and soon countless brooms are hauling in water faster and faster.

In no time at all, the workshop is swamped and overflowing, and Mickey, tossed in the waves, can barely keep from drowning. When all seems lost, the sorcerer returns, sees what mischief has been done, and without a word he breaks the spell, calms the waters, and lets the flood recede.

Here's the point: You can't stop what you think and feel, at least not for long. If you try really hard, you can stuff your

Inner Judge and tell yourself you're in control. But all your effort only makes your Inner Judge stronger and stronger, until it comes to control *you*. Your Inner Judge is persistent and determined—like the broom, it doesn't know when to stop—and it fights back until it becomes the dominant voice in your head. And its endless negativity only makes your challenge worse, deepens your fears, cravings, angers, and so on, until you feel awash and drowning in your problems.

So stop trying to stop. If, instead, you'll recognize your Inner Judge, embrace it as a useful, enduring part of you, and allow it to have its say, you'll soon quiet its voice. And then you'll be one step closer to hearing the wise, calming, healing voice deep inside you, the voice of the sorcerer within, your inner TruSage.

CHAPTER 3

Resolve Your Challenge

H ave you ever seen or heard about the 1993 movie *Groundhog Day?* The tagline in the trailer is "He's having the worst day of his life . . . over and over again." And that's the clever and fascinating premise of the story.

Pittsburgh TV weatherman Phil Connors (Bill Murray) is none too happy about being sent (again, for the fourth year in a row) to cover the annual Groundhog Day celebration in the little town of Punxsutawney, Pennsylvania. Trapped that night by a blizzard, he awakens the next morning only to discover that it's Groundhog Day all over again. The day unfolds in exactly the same way, and then the same thing happens the following morning . . . and then again . . . and again. No matter what he does, or how hard he tries to break the loop, Connors seems doomed to wake up each morning in the same place, and to relive the same day, every day, for the rest of his life.

This is just what it feels like for people who are trapped in their personal challenges and stuck in the fifteenth row. No matter how hard they try to make positive changes in their lives, their "solutions" just loop them back into their problems. They wake up in the same old movie, enacting the same old patterns and listening to the same old self-criticism, every day, on and on, for years, sometimes for life.

But this doesn't have to be the end of the story.

So far, in the Find Your Voice process you've learned how to experience your challenge (Step 1) and how to work with your Inner Judge (Step 2). Now in Step 3, you're going to learn how to resolve your challenge in new ways that will work for you, and that will keep on working.

Here's how the four clients from Step 2 got on with their challenges:

Jeff learned to lighten up about his porn craving and be less critical of his secret life. This let him feel "more grown up," while still keeping the best parts of being a kid. He said, "I've begun to see myself with different eyes," and he knew that "the answers had come from underneath."

Kris, too, said she found "a whole new way of looking at things." For the first time in her life, she went from feeling inadequate to feeling capable, empowered, and "much more caring about myself." And as she began to take better care of herself, her need for cigarettes eased away "on its own."

Rick said that when he began "listening to my intuition," he recognized what a huge role repression and self-criticism had played in locking him up in anxiety, and he understood how important it was for him to accept himself and love himself "no matter what." With more self-love, he was able to face his fears, and he began to realize just how powerless they were, "like the Wizard of Oz," as he put it, "when you look behind the curtain."

And Sandy said she was learning to "listen to my own needs," and this meant becoming "more self-respectful—not selfish—but self-respectful." As she came to respect and love herself, she began to treat herself differently, to support herself, to "be there" for herself, whenever she felt low or wanted a drink. For the first time in a long time, she was living in a "hopeful, much more positive" way, and she felt she was finally "moving on in life."

"Moving on in life" is really a three-step process, and the third step is the move you make to the last row of the theater, where you're able to see your life movie, and your fifteenth row Critic, with new eyes. It's there, in the last row, that you begin to see the bigger picture of your life and your challenge; that you find new perspectives, make new discoveries, gain new insights and understandings; that you become more spontaneous, more present, more creative and intuitive; that you learn how right it feels to be kind to yourself, compassionate, and to treat yourself with unconditional love, trust, and respect.

All this happens because it's there, in the last row, that you begin to hear the wisdom of your true, authentic voice, the voice of your deepest instinct for health and happiness.

The Sky Above

A great way to start seeing your challenge with different eyes—seeing the bigger picture—is by taking a new look at the world around you and setting yourself and your challenge into this larger context. By exploring the edges of your experience, you just might come to realize that the problem you thought was so enormous, important, and permanent in your life is really rather small, bashful, and temporary.

So, first, and whenever you get the chance—every day if possible—go outside for just a minute or two and look into the sky, up and beyond the clouds, into the heavens. You'll see that the sky goes on into infinity. It never ends.

If it's nighttime, look up past the moon and stars, and focus on the vast spaces between the stars. The night sky too goes on and on, endlessly, into infinity.

Day or night, just take a few moments to look into the sky's depth. There's no specific object to stare at. You can't really look at the sky; you have to look into it. It goes on and on. There are no boundaries, no limits. It's a never-ending view. This is a powerful last-row experience: You simply look up into the sky, and as you focus, nothing at all happens. You look into the sky with innocence and openness, and you see serenity.

Your fifteenth-row Critic will probably pop up and say, "This is not rational, helpful, or valuable." Or your Inner Judge may well ask, "Where is the sky?" "It's empty out there."

Thank your Inner Judge/Critic for sharing its opinions, of course, but then come back to looking up into the sky, into its depths, just looking without judging, thinking, or analyzing. When you look into the unlimited openness, your last-row self knows there's no need to verbalize, to talk to yourself, or to describe it in any way. If you start thinking, start putting words to the experience, you know you've slipped into the fifteenth row.

But when you focus on the vastness of the sky and see the limitless, never-ending freedom of the universe, you feel the same thing inside—you feel an amazing sense of freedom inside at the same time. The outer amazement becomes the inner amazement

When you make this move to the last row, you immediately feel calm, serene, at peace, in the flow, your stress and worries disappear, the tensions in your mind evaporate. Your fifteenth row stops for a little while!

This reconnecting with your last-row self is something you can experience a few times a day—or night—for a few moments, and it can make a world of difference.

You might ask, "Can it be this simple?" Naturally, the answer is, "Yes!"

The Earth Below

Now let's come down to earth and explore the opposite edge of your world. Looking deep into the sky above is a wonderfully freeing last-row experience, but so is feeling your deep connection to the earth below.

To get another view of the bigger picture, I want you to go outside and take a short walk, or you can stay in your house or office, sitting in a comfortable chair, and imagine taking a walk outside. Outside or inside, be sure to notice how beautiful the trees are, and certainly it feels as if you're seeing the trees with different eyes and with new clarity. Maybe you've already done your breathing; maybe you're doing your breathing as you walk. Either way, walking and breathing, or breathing and walking, you notice that the trees you see (or in your mind's eye) are as much a part of existence as you are, and you're as full of life as they are.

Next, find a place to sit down, on the grass or a bench (or in your chair), and put your feet flat on the ground or the floor. Change positions if you have to, but make sure you get both feet flat on the ground or the floor. And as you do this, be aware of the feelings in your feet, give all your attention to the feelings in your feet. Your heels, the balls of your feet, your toes. See if you can tell where your feet are touching the ground or floor, and where there are spaces. Whether you have shoes on, or socks, or bare feet, just be aware of your feet. Try to be your feet.

And as you put all your attention, all your focus, into your feet, you may notice some interesting sensations, maybe some heaviness, maybe some tingling. Just allow whatever's happening to happen. There's nothing you have to try to do; there's nothing you have to change. You're learning how to take the best possible care of yourself, from the ground up.

Now, with your feet flat on the ground or floor, it's time to imagine that your feet actually have roots going into the earth. Feel the roots coming out of the bottom of your feet into the earth; they go down into the earth maybe a foot, two feet, three feet, four feet, five feet. Depending on how old or young you feel as a tree, allow the roots to come right out of your feet, go right into the earth, and feel them branching out into the earth. And you have a feeling of being grounded, of being connected to the earth, and certainly of feeling rooted deeply into the experience of life.

So here's another way to move yourself to the last row: Just put all your awareness into your feet and feel the roots coming right out *of your feet into the earth. You can do this inside or outside, sitting or standing. You can carry this with you everywhere you go. Feel it, visualize it—let yourself get intensely in touch with life—and you'll enter a beautiful state of inner peace.*

The healing power of feeling rooted in the earth is that you're continually re-connecting yourself to what really matters. You're alive. You're part of the life around you. You're deeper and more firmly grounded than your challenge.

Learning to *See*

In most cases, seeing yourself and your challenge with "new eyes" means literally learning to *see* again. Living with chronic pain, cravings, fear, sadness, and so on works to dim your vision. Locked into your challenge, you live out of habit, marching to the drumbeat of your social/family programming, or your Inner Judge, and the power of the present moment and the beauty of the world are lost to you.

All of this is like being a robot. It's mechanical. It's living blind. You're so familiar with the pictures on your walls that you don't see them anymore. You're so used to the face staring back at you from the mirror that you no longer see what you look like. You look but you don't *see*.

As If for the Very First Time

But you can become alive again, alert, your eyes filled with freshness. Just take a few moments to practice seeing yourself and your world as if for the very first time.

Start with your body. Take a moment to look at your hands. Really see your hands, the nails, the lines, the knuckles. See them as if for the very first time. Look at your feet, your legs, your arms, your stomach—all, as if you've never seen them before. If it's convenient, go to a mirror and look at your face as if you're meeting yourself for the first time. Look at your eyes in particular; if you really see your eyes, they'll be filled with freshness.

Now move into your relationships. If you're with friends or family, or if you're at work, see your loved ones and the people around you as if for the very first time. Stop living with your eyes dulled from habit. See your spouse, your partner, your children (if any), your parents (if still alive), your friends, your boss, and your co-workers as if you're meeting them for the very first time, as if they're people you're just getting to know. Your eyes will sparkle.

You can do this with simple objects, too. Wherever you are, find an object and focus your attention on it. It might be something you look at all the time (like a clock) or something you hardly ever notice (like a lamp). Look at the object as a whole thing, with its own unique properties, qualities, its own special history and character. Now look at the object as if you've just discovered it and are seeing it for the very first time. Keep concentrating on this one object. After a few moments, you may find that you're seeing the object with new eyes, and realizing that it's quite amazing in its own right.

And you can look to nature. Step outside for a few moments and look at the natural world around you. See the clouds in the sky, a bird flying, a bed of flowers, a tree close by or a mountain in the distance—all as if for the very first time. Try to see a sunrise or sunset whenever you can. These never happen the same way twice.

Make a point of seeing yourself and your world as if for the very first time. See if you can make this a continuous attitude. This can change things. When you start seeing more clearly, more truly, you'll begin living more in the present, more spontaneously and creatively.

And you may begin to see yourself more clearly, too, and realize this powerful truth: that you're absolutely and uniquely yourself—you're 100 percent *you*. Life never creates anything less than that. There has never been a person like you before. There will never be another person like you again. Nobody's fingerprints are like yours; nobody's eyes are like yours; nobody has the same voice as you. You don't have to try to be yourself. You don't have to do anything special. You're already special. It's in your soul. It's your true, authentic last-row self.

Your Seven Senses

Gaining this fresh perspective on yourself and your life is more than just a matter of seeing. Vision may be our dominant sense, and our eyes may be the "window to the soul," as the saying goes, but engaging your other senses is also enormously important in helping you make the move to the last row.

After you've taken a fresh look at yourself and your world, try focusing on your other senses, one after the other. For this technique, I want you to close your eyes; this will help you get free from distracting visuals.

When you have a chance, take a time out from your busy day and find a place where you can be comfortable. If you sit down or lie down, first feel the support of the chair, cushions, or mattress. Notice how soft or firm these are, and where they touch your body and where they don't. Also, be aware of all the textures and temperatures surrounding you: the feel of your clothing, the coolness or warmth of the air on your face, the slight pressure of your lips touching. Just let yourself observe and consider any sort of physical contact. You are your skin.

Next, listen to all the sounds around you. Notice outside sounds: the birds, the wind, children playing down the block, or maybe some sounds that bother you, like the drone of a plane overhead, or the barking of a neighbor's dog. Notice inside sounds: a clock ticking, your furnace kicking on, or a light bulb faintly humming. Listen inside you, too: to your breathing, to your heart beating. Even if you can't hear anything, listen to the sound of silence. You are your ears.

Now, smell the fragrances: the pine tree in the yard, the flowers in the vase, the fragrance of your makeup or after-shave, the lingering smells of cooking or clean clothing, of fireplace ashes or fresh air. Some people say that life itself has a fragrance. You are your nose.

Can you taste anything? Any trace of the coffee from breakfast or the sandwich from lunch? Any taste of lip balm or lipstick? If not, just lick your lips and taste the saltiness, the moisture, the dryness. You are your tongue.

Not many people know that you have two more senses. That's right . . . seven senses (and you thought you had only five). So next pay attention to what people often call your "sixth sense," your intuition. What's your intuition sensing right now about your self-care? What's your "gut feeling" about your challenge? What's your heart saying about becoming so keenly aware of your physical sensations? You are your intuition.

And, finally, what's your seventh sense, your sense of humor, saying? Are you smiling or amused? Can you laugh a little with yourself, about the awkwardness of learning something new?

About the silly side of your problems? About the resistances that are arising? You are your laughter.

The truth is, to a large extent you've been shaped by your past, programmed by your experiences, imprisoned by your habits. Once you've lived with any habit for a long time—experienced habitually any pain, any craving, any fear, anything at all—it takes root in your body. It's in your chemistry. It becomes automatic.

But when you learn how to see again, but also to feel, listen, smell, taste, intuit, and laugh, you step out of your programming, and for a few moments you gain a new perspective on life. By tuning in to your seven senses, you connect directly with your last-row self—with the power of the moment and with the wise voice of your intuition—and this helps you discover new, more creative solutions to your challenge.

De-programming Your Challenge

Here's a short meditation that addresses this whole idea of how re-activating your physical senses can help in de-programming your challenge.

Get yourself comfortable, take three deep, cleansing breaths, and read the following lines slowly and quietly to yourself; you'll move right into your healing inner voice.

When you walk, walk slowly . . . notice.
The breeze, you'll feel,
Lightly brushes your skin.
When you look, look with clarity . . . observe.
The trees, you'll see,

Are greener than they've ever been.
When you listen, listen closely . . . attend.
The birds, you'll hear,
Sing more sweetly than you can imagine.
Learn something, too.
Learn to focus on the moment at hand.
Let the moment be your purpose.
Your Inner Judge, resisting any change,
Will try to block the way,
Saying, "You'll never be happy," and "It's too hard."
Don't repress or it will fight back stronger.
Just observe and be polite.
Never say, "I hate you, go away!"
Say, "Yes, I hear you. Thank you.
But I choose not to follow you right now."

The Third Eye

Let's turn now from the outer world of the physical senses, and explore the other edge, the inner world accessed by your "sixth sense," or intuition. Looking inside is no more difficult than looking outside, particularly if you know how to see with your third eye.

You might have heard about the third eye. You have two regular eyes and they're for seeing outward. But you also have a third eye, right in between your eyebrows, and it's for seeing inward. In Buddhist and Hindu mysticism, and also in the Jewish Kabbalah, the third eye is a symbol of enlightenment and spiritual transcendence. It's been variously referred to as the "eye of knowledge," as the seat of the "teacher inside," as the "sixth chakra" or "brow chakra," which is the wisdom center, and as the "tenth gate," which leads to myriad inner realms of higher consciousness. More commonly, it's known by the phrase "the mind's eye."

To some, the third eye is more than a metaphor. For centuries, it's been known that between the two hemispheres of the brain lies a small gland called the pineal gland, and it's been suggested that this is in fact the mythical, mystical third eye. René Descartes, the seminal seventeenth-century French rational philosopher and mathematician, studied the pineal gland and called it "the seat of the soul." Modern medical science has discovered that the pineal gland (which is partially dormant in adults) secretes melatonin, the hormone that makes us light sensitive, and so affects our circadian rhythms of waking and sleeping. Maybe this accounts for the ancient association between the third eye and enlightenment or inner awakening.

But whether symbol or science, the third eye does seem to close up for many of us when we become adults. Caught up in the "busyness" of our lives and our personal challenges, we don't take the time to look inside.

And yet the third eye is not blind. It's there, fully functional, and can be opened at any moment. All you have to do is learn *how*. Here's a method I came across in my study of meditation.

Close your eyes and focus your attention just in the middle of your eyebrows. Give all your attention to your third eye, as if looking at it with your two eyes. Your attention will be quickly absorbed, drawn immediately inward—the third eye is a magnet for attention—and your two eyes will soon become fixed, as in deep meditation. It's amazing how quickly and how fully aware you can become of this one small part of your body. It's as if the third eye is hungry for awareness. It's been hungry for years and years. If you give it your full attention, you're nourishing it, and it opens wide.

Once your awareness is focused on your third eye, you begin to see your challenge from a wonderful new perspective. Instead of blindly, automatically identifying with your craving, or your fear, or your anger, or your Inner Critic—instead of getting stuck in your challenge, or in the fifteenth row—you begin to see your thoughts, feelings, and criticisms from the last row, and so with more distance, more objectivity, and more compassion.

Through the third eye, you see your thoughts, feelings, and criticisms like clouds drifting across the sky, or like people passing on the sidewalk. You're sitting at your window, maybe on the third or fourth floor, looking up at the sky above or down at the street below, but you don't personally identify with what you see. You're curious and caring, but aloof at the same time, detached, centered in yourself, an observer, a witness, watching your thoughts, feelings, and criticisms as they come and go.

By practicing this technique, you're training your third eye to look inward, and in the process, you're becoming more aware, more relaxed, and more present. As I've said, change happens first on the inside and then on the outside. So look inside and see things with a different eye—your third eye.

Body, Mind, Heart, and Soul

Exploring your inner world is more than just looking inside; it also means listening to your inner wisdom—your voice— and hearing what it has to say about resolving your challenge.

I recommended the Committee Meeting technique in Steps 1 and 2 to help you manage all the loud, chattering, conflicting voices in your head—the voices of your pain, your craving, your anxiety, your Inner Judge, and all the rest.

Remember, you might seat many committee members, or just a few—it really doesn't matter. As long as they're all acknowledged, accepted, and expressed, you'll be open to new learning, new experiences, and new perspectives. And you'll be able to arrive at new answers in a committee report that takes all opinions and attitudes into account.

Here's a different sort of Committee Meeting, one designed not to clear your head of chatter but to connect you directly to your healing inner voice.

First, take a piece of paper and at the top write down these four words: Body, Mind, Heart, and Intuition. Next, get as comfortable as you can. Focus on your breathing, on the rise and fall of each breath, and notice that your breathing has a rhythm, in and out, just like the waves at the beach. Accept your breathing as it is, big or small, deep or shallow, and then pause at the turning points, just for a moment, just at the moment of quiet, the moment of peace . . .

Now, with your pencil in your non-dominant hand, I want you to scan your body *from the bottom of your feet all the way to the top of your head, and ask yourself: How does your body feel about your challenge? Do you feel any tension? Any tightness? Feel any stress anywhere? You know, maybe you feel kind of clenched in your stomach or tight in the back of your neck. You're doodling, scribbling, drawing pictures, writing words. If your body could talk, if your body had a voice of its own about your challenge, what would your body say? I feel . . . here's where my tension is . . . here's where I hurt . . . this is where my discomfort is.*

Give your body a voice and express whatever your body is feeling about your goals. And it may be things you've been noticing for a long time or may be brand-new stuff that you're just getting in touch with now. Let your body express itself. No more repressing in your body. No more pushing things down in your body. This is your body talking. This is your body language. Take a couple of minutes and let your body have its say. Let your body express itself. This is your opportunity to say "Yes" to your body. Whatever you feel, whatever you want to say, right onto the paper with your non-dominant hand. That's right.

And when you're ready, use your breathing as a bridge to your mind, *your thinking, your intelligence, your ideas, your theories. What does your mind have to say about your challenge? Your mind is always thinking, and maybe you have a lot of thoughts, a lot of views, a lot of opinions. What are you thinking about? What are your ideas about your issue? What are your concerns about it? What kind of worries, doubts, reluctance, ambivalence? Any thoughts at all. Give your intelligence a voice. What does it say?*

And just allow your mind to express, to communicate, to be heard, from your head to your hand to the paper. What does your mind say? Maybe what you thought it would say, maybe more, maybe less. That's right. What does your mind say? Maybe it seems like you've been stuck in your head on this issue. Maybe you feel like you've been over-thinking it, or perhaps not thinking enough about it. I don't know. It really doesn't matter. Just allow your mind, your ideas, your thoughts, your sense, your intelligence to have a voice, to express itself about your challenge.

Focus again on your breath work, at your own pace, noticing the rise and fall of each breath, and use your breathing as the bridge to transition from your mind to your heart. *Ask yourself, how does your heart feel about your challenge? It's not literally your heart. It's your heart as a metaphor for how you* feel. *What are your feelings about your challenge? You might notice your feelings right across your chest, right in between your armpits. A lot of people say they feel closed and tight right there when they're stressed, and warm and open there when they're relaxed. What are your feelings? What are your emotions?*

If your heart had a voice and your heart could talk, what would it say about this issue? What would it say about this goal? Accept what you feel. Express what you feel. Give your heart a chance to talk. You've heard the expression "heartfelt feelings." No more pushing down. No more holding in. No more holding back. Go ahead and say everything your heart feels about this issue. That's right. Finally, you have an opportunity, right here, right now, to give your heart a voice, to express your feelings about your challenge—from the heart. Let go, let go, let go. Be all heart for yourself and give your heart a voice. From your heart to your hand to the paper. Good.

And at your own pace, with your breathing as the bridge, focusing on the rise and fall of each breath, ask yourself: What does your intuition *say about your challenge? And just allow your intuition to bubble up. First with your non-dominant hand and then with your dominant hand, what does your intuition say? You've heard from your body. You've heard from your mind. You've heard from your heart. Now what does your intuition say? Most people think of their intuition as in their gut, kind of a gut feeling. But really it's your deepest self, your true, authentic self, that secret, sacred part of you—some call it your soul—that's brimming with wisdom and creative personal insight. The poet William Wordsworth, for example, described intuition in these lines: "with an eye made quiet by the power of harmony/And the deep power of joy," we "become a living soul" and "see into the life of things."*

And so, from this last-row perspective, big picture, comfortably detached, loving, and compassionate self, what bubbles up? What comes to you as the best resolution of your challenge? Just take your time, be patient, and wonder what your intuition is going to reveal. It might be exactly what you expected. It might be completely different. It might be very simple. It might be quite complex. Anything at all. From the last row, writing with your non-dominant hand, doodling, drawing pictures, what's your best solution to this problem? Remember, this is the truest you. This soul, this intuition, this healing inner voice is closer than maybe you've ever been to your inner wisdom. From the last row, what's the best solution?

Feel how freeing it is to let your intuition go. You can trust that when you are 100 percent about giving your body a voice, and 100 percent about giving your mind a voice, and 100 percent about giving your heart a voice, then the voice of your intuition will come shining through with 100 percent. And this is what's meant by being whole, by being your true self, by honoring yourself, accepting yourself, body, mind, heart, and soul. You've heard that before. Listen and be guided by your own body, mind, heart, and soul.

One last word about Committee Meetings: If you do your committee work for all your big issues and hold meetings on a regular basis, one day you'll be done with them. After a while, the process will become second nature, and you'll do the awareness, accepting, expressing, and resolving without even thinking about it. It's like when you were a child learning how to read. First you studied the alphabet: You memorized and practiced the letters, and started to sound out words. But pretty soon you just knew how to read; the process simply became a natural part of your consciousness. That's exactly what happens with the Committee Meeting technique. At first it takes some time and effort, but soon it becomes internalized and you're doing it unconsciously.

Time Traveling

Exploring the far opposite edges of your world—above and below, outside and inside—has helped you see the bigger picture of your challenge and feel centered in yourself. But there's another polarity—past and future—that can add the dimension of time to this larger context. By taking the ACE Questionnaire in Step 1 and the Family Origins Quiz in Step 2, you've already experienced the healing power of looking into your past and accepting and expressing the hurts you found there. But your memory work can be even more powerful, even more freeing and centering, when you couple it with a creative, intuitive, last-row look into the future.

To show you what I mean, let's start by seeing how a little time traveling can help you resolve your negative feelings about other people.

So take a few moments, get comfortable, maybe take a couple of deep, satisfying breaths, and . . .

Let yourself imagine that you're in the last row of the theater, watching your Inner Critic in the fifteenth row, and both of you are watching the movie of your life. Only this time you see on the screen a person you know quite well, and who annoys you, who bothers you no end, maybe a colleague at work, maybe your boss, maybe a neighbor, maybe somebody on TV. That's right, someone in your life whom you're quick to criticize.

While you're watching this person acting in your movie, acting as they always do, annoying you, driving you up a wall, imagine that the screen gets wavy for a second and there's a flashback to this person's childhood, maybe to when she was five or six years old. Good. See if you can tell what the person looked like as a youngster; listen to what she sounded like; imagine what her home life was like, her parents, her brothers or sisters. Give yourself some time to make the scene as detailed as possible.

The screen gets wavy again, and the movie flashes forward to a time when the person you judge so severely is old, maybe eighty or eighty-five years old. Here, again, see if you can imagine what this person will look like in her later years, what she will sound like, who will be left in her life, what she'll do with her time. That's right.

The screen gets wavy once again, and you return to the present day. Look at this annoying person, at how she is now, acting in your movie, and see if you can get a glimpse of the five-year-old in the present person. Maybe the nose is the same, maybe a look in the eye, maybe how she walks. See the child hiding in the grown-up. Now look again and see if you can find the eighty-year-old in the present person. It's the same person, only maybe the shoulders have stooped, the voice has thinned, the hair has gone grey, and the walk has slowed. See what time will do to this person.

And now from the last row, whenever you're ready, ask yourself, after having this experience, how do you feel about the movie? How do you feel about the person you criticize? And how do you feel about your Inner Critic? Listen as your voice comes up with new answers.

As you know, you mustn't try to stop judging people; that only makes matters worse. But seeing people in the context of their whole life, from childhood to old age, lets you go deeper and learn to be more understanding and forgiving.

And here's a secret: If you can do this with other people, you can do this with yourself.

Embrace Your Past

No matter how difficult your memories are, no matter how many troubling, disturbing voices from childhood you have in your head, you can understand yourself, accept yourself—even love yourself—just as you are. I want you to find a quiet place where you can get comfortable, take a couple of deep breaths, and prepare yourself to take a long, relaxing walk.

As you begin, notice that you're on a great, beautiful pathway, wide enough for plenty of people to pass, but that you're the only one walking today. And as you continue walking and going down a little hill, you can see the graceful trees growing and all the branches where they spread out over the pathway creating a kind of green, leafy canopy. A truly beautiful place. You can see the birds, but you can hear them more than see them. You can see the blue sky through the branches of the trees; you can feel the sun's warmth. Just an absolutely perfect day. And here you are, with this place to yourself, and it's really safe, really beautiful. Mother Nature has been very generous to this spot.

And as you continue walking, you notice that way, way down the path there's a very big tree. It looks like it might be the biggest tree in the whole forest. And you're interested in it and walk toward it, and you notice some squirrels in the distance running up the branches. The clouds are looking really pretty up there, way up in the sky. It's one of those days that you just love because it's so comfortable, nature is so bounteous.

And you're continuing to walk toward the tree, and as you get closer and closer, you realize there's a small child sitting right at the base of the tree, down by the roots of the tree. Curious. And so you walk closer and closer, and as you do, you realize that the child looks familiar. And as you get closer and closer, and get right up to this child, you realize this child is you.

What a powerful moment. And then, instinctively, moved by the force of deep self-love, you and the child reach out to each other and hold each other, and hug each other, and you feel the closeness and the oneness, maybe in a way neither of you has felt for a long, long time. You both have this great feeling of love, and care, and deep connection.

And now a conversation can happen where the grown-up you says everything you want to say to the child, any advice, any encouragement, any regrets, any words of forgiveness or support or understanding. And, of course, the young child listens, totally open to whatever you want to say.

And naturally, the young child wants to say some things to you, some questions, some sorrows, some secrets, some hopes and dreams. And, of course, you listen, fully open to the child's words. That's right. What a beautiful conversation.

Soon you realize the sun is getting low, and it's time to walk back up the little hill, back to where you started. And as you do, you feel different, more connected to yourself if that's possible. More alive, and refreshed, and relaxed if that's possible, with a great sense of relief and encouragement. And walking back, you notice even more colors, and more trees, and shapes in the clouds, and just a world of difference in how much more clearly you see things.

This is a great healing experience that you can come back to anytime. It's a powerful time of communion and communication with yourself in your wise, loving inner voice.

Embrace Your Future

But the power of this self-communication is multiplied when you can find a moment to step into your future. By imagining how you'll be in your old age, you're actually creating a relationship between your present self, troubled with your challenge, and your future self, who has lived through your trouble and can look back with the wisdom of years. The following Find Your Voice visualization allows you to develop that relationship with love and respect.

Get into your relaxed, receptive mood with your breathing, maybe with some stretching, maybe some clenching and releasing (Entrance and Exit) . . .

Imagine yourself going on another long walk, following a path that's in front of you, up a little hill, and you're seeing the beautiful trees, noticing that even though you can't see the roots of the trees, you know they're down there, and that's a really solid feeling. And you're noticing the clouds up in the sky and just watching the clouds go by one at a time, just as you can watch your own thoughts go by like clouds in the sky—here one comes . . . there it goes. And as you're watching the clouds, you can put a thought into each cloud and just watch them come and watch them go. They're always temporary. That's one thing you know for sure.

And you notice way up the path, sitting at the base of a magnificent old tree, there's a person, looks like an older person, can't really make it out from here, but you're curious, open, you have a sense of adventure, which you've been developing more and more.

And as you get closer and closer to that tree, it looks as if the person at the base of the tree is an elderly person and somebody who looks kind of familiar. And as you get closer and closer, you realize this person is you, a future you, a much older version of you, maybe seventy, eighty, or ninety, or even a hundred years old.

And with this recognition, you walk right up and reach down, and the older you rises and reaches out, and you clasp hands, and you embrace each other. A magical moment, a great feeling of closeness. And you hold each other in an embrace filled with love, and care, and compassion, that's right, filled with understanding, and acceptance.

And now a conversation can happen. Whatever you want to say to your older self, any questions you want to ask, that's fine. And, of course, your older self is compassionate, and friendly, and open, and listening.

And then whatever your older self wants to say to you, any advice, encouragement, important changes you can make, challenges you'll face, you're open, and you listen. That's right. And now as the conversation flows back and forth, you're pleasantly surprised by your openness and your receptiveness to each other.

And only after you feel satisfied with the dialogue, whenever you feel satisfied and have some new ideas, then you say good-bye and begin the journey back down to where you started, seeing things with different eyes, more clearly, open to new learning. That's right. Really noticing where you're going to give your attention from now on, and feeling like you've just given yourself a beautiful gift that you can bring along into the future.

You can enjoy your life more and more, largely free from the emotional or physical challenge that has so long imprisoned you. But it all begins with how you feel about yourself, and how you treat yourself. Be respectful, be supportive, be caring, be compassionate, be understanding with yourself, listen to your commitments. Learn to care for yourself the way you would care for someone else, maybe a dear friend, whom you really love and respect. Nourish yourself that way and you'll grow into the future you've dreamed of.

If You've Done One Thing Well

Now let's narrow your focus and explore a time frame—recent past, near future—that's closer to your life right now.

A huge hurdle for most of us when we try to deal with personal problems is how to overcome our thoughts of past failure. We want to find answers and make positive changes, but all too often we let the memory of our failings undermine our confidence and sabotage our efforts. It almost seems that negative experiences and emotions have more lasting emotional power than positive experiences and emotions—that we let failure and disappointment affect us more deeply than success and satisfaction.

So to make your best progress in resolving any personal challenge, you need to learn how to build on what you've done well in the past. Here's a Find Your Voice technique that will help you utilize your past successes to help resolve your present challenge.

Go ahead (if you haven't already), focus on your breathing, and maybe notice your turning points to help you relax. Sometimes it's helpful to ask yourself this question: How relaxed can I feel right now? Repeat that question to yourself (and not out loud) ten or twenty times until you really feel a change and a positive click, a positive "yes." How relaxed can I feel right now? Take all the time you need to make yourself feel as comfortable and relaxed as possible . . .

I want you to focus, using your third eye perhaps, on one thing in your life you've done really well. Maybe you've been a good friend, maybe a good parent, maybe it's playing tennis, maybe working with people or with your computer, maybe gardening or cooking or being open to new ideas. Anything from A to Z, from your adolescence to your adulthood. Whether it seems more playful than important, or more serious than fun, it really doesn't matter. I just want you to focus on one thing you've done really well, because if you've done one thing well, you can do this well, too.

Now, whatever you're thinking about right now, whatever you're picturing in your mind, whatever you're feeling in your body, focus on this one thing you've done well and be as specific as possible with yourself about the details of how you learned to do it.

Naturally, you had to be an amateur to begin with—you had to start somewhere. But how did you go from knowing next to nothing about it to becoming good at it? What was the process? What did you have to do to get good at this one thing? What were the steps? What was the formula? Did you read a book? Did you need a coach? Did you write about it? Did you talk to other people about it? How much time and energy did you put into it? How long did it take? Did you have any breakthroughs along the way? How exactly did you learn to do this one thing really well?

Remember details that maybe you've forgotten, or that you haven't thought about in a long time. Get into it, be that age, live in that house, be at that job, and remember and actually re-experience, re-live how you went from knowing very little or nothing about something to doing it really well. Use all your senses. See it. Feel it. Hear the conversations. Smell the place. Remember the taste you had for learning this new thing and becoming really proficient, really good at it. You might be surprised about some things. I don't know. But take these minutes to remember the steps or stages. That's right. See how you did it. See what had to happen. See what you had to do.

Okay, when you have enough information, enough details, and you can feel it—you're not just thinking about it, but you can feel it—start to apply this process, this formula, to your challenge, to your self-care and positive transformation. What do you need to do? What are the steps? What's the process? You already have this inside of you. You've been doing it for a long time, and now you're applying what already works for you to your present goal, your number-one priority. Do you need to do more reading? Do you need to do more practicing? Do you need to do it every day? Do you need to talk to other people? Whatever you did to become good at that one thing, apply all of that formula to your challenge right now.

Enjoy the process. Enjoy the journey. You're discovering that if you've done one thing well, you can do this well, too. Take a couple of more minutes and focus on what it took for you to do that one thing well, same formula, same steps, same process, and apply it to what's really important to you and what you're working on now. Stay with it. Stay with it. Be playful about it. Be serious about it. Have fun with it. Be focused. Remember the whole premise here. That's right. If you've done one thing well, you can do this well, too.

You've been opening up a lot of new doors, developing a lot of new resources, finding new answers inside yourself. Take another few minutes with this before you finish. You already know that often, just before you finish, something really important clicks inside. And from a deep place, you hear a voice telling you something that you're always going to remember.

So now, at your own pace, when you feel really good about what you've done here, start to finish up. And as you've probably already guessed, go back to your breathing. Go back to focusing on the rise and fall of each breath. That's right. Accept your breathing as it is and pause with awareness at the turning points. That's right. Finish up with this, because your breathing is always a bridge to the last row and your true, authentic self.

Everyone has problems and failures in life, but no one is born with crippling self-criticism, negative programming, self-destructive habits, self-doubts, and self-limits. You've been given these things, been taught them while growing up, and they've become huge stumbling blocks in the road to realizing your potential for positive growth. With the Find Your Voice process, you can remove these blocks—undo what's been done to you—and get yourself back on the road to health and happiness.

Hopes and Dreams

Now, once again, reverse engines and take some time to explore your near future. Resolutions, after all, tend to look to the future. (That's what New Year's resolutions are all about.) You need to take past factors into account, of course, but you make resolutions with an eye to the future, focusing on your goals, your intentions, your hopes and dreams, on the way you *want* to be.

This is a perfect time to take out your journal and describe what you expect of your life. How do you want it to go? What changes do you want to experience? Write down everything you can about your desires, your intentions, your passions, and your commitments. Be specific. Make plans that are reachable, doable, and imagine your sense of accomplishment as you complete them. And definitely make them fun. How do you want to look and feel, physically, mentally, emotionally, or even spiritually? What's it going to be like to manage your challenge effectively, to quiet your Inner Judge, to see yourself and your life from the last row?

Focus with an open mind, and an open heart, and a total commitment to developing your potential. Alternate between your dominant and non-dominant hands—dominant for your thoughts and ideas, non-dominant for your feelings and fantasies. Write down the new ways in which you'll take care of yourself. Write about the new things that you want to add to your life, any new activities, new feelings, new behaviors, new opportunities, even new perspectives.

Start by focusing on what you'd like to accomplish in the next twenty-four hours. Maybe it's something as simple as feeling relaxed and confident. Maybe it's something about your challenge. I just want you to take a few minutes to describe to yourself what you want to feel in the next twenty-four hours. Maybe how you want to handle a certain situation, maybe a certain person, maybe yourself. And so you watch the movie of your life as you want it to go, get a feeling for what's happening in your movie, listen to the dialogue, watch it from the last row of the theater, how you want things to go for the next twenty-four hours. That's right. You're learning how to see your life with new eyes and take the best possible care of yourself.

As you work with this technique, you can write in your journal about what you want one month from now, three months from now, then six months, one year from now, even five years from now. What about ten years from now? You see, you're making plans to make your life freer and happier. You're writing about how you'll deal with problems. You're writing about being calm in rough times. You're writing about resting fully when you go to bed at night. You're writing about how great it feels to make a transformation from your very core. You can write about a renewed love for life, about flexibility, about being open to exploring. You can write about pacing yourself, self-acceptance, self-love, health, enjoyment, and freedom.

You're writing in your journal about disentangling from your old, unwanted habits, about your new commitments, about making better sense of your life, about your ability to see things with different eyes, about your ever-evolving nature. Writing about being proactive instead of reactive. Writing about living each day fully and about breathing and relaxing a little bit every day. Writing about integrating your new feelings, your self-respect, and your self-acceptance.

Maybe you're even writing poetry or drawing, doodling. Or maybe you're considering the script changes you want to make in your life movie. Go ahead and rewrite the script of how you want things to go. Change the plot; change the dialogue. From this moment forward, I want. . . . That's right. How do you want things to go from now on?

Be assured that if you're open to new ideas and options, and if you nourish your intentions to be healthy, happy, to take care of yourself, to befriend yourself, even to love yourself, you can become the author of your own future.

Both Hands on the Wheel

However, let's not forget that the real focus of the Find Your Voice process is on the present, on becoming happy and healthy in your life just as it is right now. Exploring your past and future is valuable in its own right: It's good to learn from the past and to strive for future goals. But more than this, exploring your past and future has a magical way of centering you in the *present*—a place of power in which you immediately feel relaxation, balance, and peace, a place of resolution in which you hear the spontaneous voice of your inner wisdom.

Here's an easy way to remember that your real objective is living as much as possible right here, right now, in the present moment.

When you drive your car, you sit behind the steering wheel, you look where you're going, and you check the rearview mirror occasionally to see where you've been. So when you drive, just as in daily life, the future is always out in front of you, the past is always behind you, and you're right here, right now, in the present, with both hands on the wheel.

Now if you go through life always focused on what's coming two miles, three miles down the road, and next week, next month, too far in the future, you lose sight of where you are, and you make a lot of mistakes. Or if you're thinking about the past and staring into the rearview mirror, you can't see what's right in front of you, and you bump and crash into things all the time. The same with driving, the same with life. So the future is always in front of you, the past is always behind you, and you're always in the present, with both hands on the wheel.

Anytime you're driving, you can remind yourself of this. And anytime in your daily life when you start to get too stressed out about future things or past things, you can remember that it's wise to be concerned about what's down the road as long as you keep in mind that it's two or three miles out there in the future. And it's valuable to check the rearview mirror every once in a while, but you don't want to be staring into it.

So here you are, in the present, the future in front of you, the past behind you. And you know the more you can accept your life as it is right now, the more you can live in the present moment—even if it's a moment of challenge—the happier you'll feel, the more freedom you'll feel, and the more easily you'll move to the last row and connect to your true, authentic voice.

By the way, this is exactly what Phil Connors learns in *Groundhog Day*. As he slowly accepts the fact that there is no yesterday or tomorrow—that *today* is all he has—he begins to discover what's really important in life: living with a heart full of love, and treating himself and others with compassion and generosity. When he has truly learned this lesson and is ready to move on in life, one night the calendar shifts and he awakens to a new day.

Drawing on Your Experience

One of the most powerful ways of exploring the edges of your experience is through art. Take drawing, for example. Any form of drawing—painting, sketching, even doodling—is a direct channel to your spontaneous, creative, intuitive mind. Drawing switches you out of your programmed perspective and allows you to see with new eyes, letting you connect more easily with the bigger "picture" of yourself and your challenge. Freed for the moment from your old familiar voices, it's as if you're expressing yourself in a new, non-verbal language, and new thoughts and feelings—and new solutions—suddenly become available to you. By giving yourself permission to do some drawing, you find a new voice of wisdom and healing.

The effects can be amazing.

Sarah, for example, was seven years old when her father died. She was crushed with sadness and grief, and she also mysteriously began suffering from asthma and headaches. Her mother brought Sarah to see me, and right away I taught her some breathing and relaxation techniques, and these helped a great deal.

But Sarah's real breakthrough came when I asked her to draw some pictures about how she felt about losing her dad.

In one especially poignant drawing, she was on the top of a mountain, with her dad in a cloud nearby, so she could talk with him. Expressing her feelings in this new way let Sarah be consoled and accept her father's death. And her physical symptoms (which were really signals) immediately eased and soon disappeared.

Terrible and Terrific

Here's a Find Your Voice technique that will let you get to the last row through the medium of drawing. Also, it's another example of how looking at the opposite edges of your experience helps you find a healing center.

Now, don't hold back because you feel you have no talent for drawing or because you haven't been to art school. You don't need a special gift or special training—all you need is a willingness to try something new and creative. As in Sarah's case, even a child can do this.

So, first, go to a drugstore and buy some drawing paper and a box of crayons, colored pencils, or colored ink markers. Or better yet, try to find some finger paints like you used in kindergarten. (This will help you become a kid again.) Then, find a private, quiet location to make some art.

Breathe deeply, and when you're ready, remember a really terrible scene in which your challenge really got the better of you. Let yourself remember vividly, and in great detail, how miserable you felt in your pain, craving, fear, anger, or the like.

On your paper, draw or paint the scene. If you feel hesitant or even blocked, just get your hands moving and see what they want to do. Let your unconscious create the shapes and the figures, the features, the scenery, and the dimensions of this terrible experience. Use the colors you think best express the negative feelings you had then. Be bold with your colors—no one will see this but you.

When you've finished, look at your picture. Talk to it. Yell at it. Cry at it. Let go . . . let go . . . let go. Once you've let all that hurt and heartache out, take several deep, cleansing breaths.

Next, think of a really terrific scene in your life when you felt free of your pain, craving, fear, anger, or the like. Remember in as much detail as possible how wonderful you felt living for a time without your challenge.

On a second sheet of paper, draw or paint this happy memory. Again, get your hand moving and let it create the shapes and the figures, the features, the scenery, and the dimensions of this wonderful experience. Use the colors that you think best express the positive feelings you had then. Be joyful and playful with your colors.

When you've finished, look at your picture. Talk to it. Sing to it. Laugh with it. Dance around it. Let go . . . let go . . . let go. Finally, take several deep, satisfying breaths and listen to what your inner voice says about your challenge.

Song and Dance

The singing and dancing I just mentioned are both forms of art that make wonderful shortcuts to the last row. (Laughing is, too, and I'll explore that later.) Music creates a beautiful harmony between your body, mind, heart, and soul that frees you from your locked-in habits and—almost like a meditation or prayer— moves you into relaxation, balance, and transcendence.

So, if you know an instrument—even a little guitar or piano— take some time every day to play the music you love. Or just listen to the radio, to your own CD collection, or to your favorite downloads on your iPod. And don't be afraid to sing along. Singing to music in the car or belting it out in the shower are great ways of connecting with your voice.

Even better, turn a rhythmical piece of music up louder than usual and dance to it. Dance slow or fast—it doesn't matter. Traditional steps or free form—it doesn't matter. Just let your unconscious say all it has to say through your body.

Rock and Roll

Let me tell you a true story of how one of my clients discovered in music and dancing a new, creative, life-changing solution to her challenge.

At thirty-five, Julie hated to look at herself in the mirror. She knew she had to lose some serious weight, but years of dieting had done no good. Julie was a waitress, and waiting tables not only put her around food all day—it also sapped her strength and motivation to exercise in the evening.

One day, Julie overheard two ladies in the restaurant make a cruel, catty joke about her size. That did it. Julie decided it was time to try a new approach to losing weight.

Julie came to see me, and as she worked with the Find Your Voice process, she discovered how much hurt and resentment she felt toward the two women who had made the joke, toward thin people in general, toward her ex-husband, and even toward her parents who had divorced when she was ten. Julie had repressed all these feelings for years, not wanting her own kids to feel the confusion and rejection she'd experienced as a child.

But now she began to write about her hurt, anger, and resentment in a personal journal each night. She also recorded information about her meals and moods, and realized that she ate more when she was lonely or bored. And she was lonely and bored so often!

As Julie learned to recognize these feelings, accept them, and express them, her enthusiasm for life began to return. Then, one night, while listening to some CDs of old 1950s rock and roll, she had an inspiration (I would call this hearing her inner voice): In her living room, she began dancing to the music and was surprised to recall the natural sense of rhythm she had once had as a girl. She was soon dancing every night, thrilled to have found a form of exercise she enjoyed.

The results were dramatic.

Julie lost sixty-five pounds in nine months. When a friend at work asked her for her secret, Julie loaned her a few CDs and promised to teach her some dance steps. It wasn't long before all the other waitresses joined in. They decided to throw a 1950s dance party at the restaurant, and the evening was such a hit that everyone agreed to make it an annual event.

Julie made more and more friends and found she was less bored and lonely. Although she was still around food all day, the excess weight stayed off. Two years later, Julie was attending a dance class three nights a week, enjoying her life, and liking the way she looked.

So play, listen, sing, dance . . . get in touch with the music in your soul, and you'll tap into depths of inner wisdom that can turn your life around.

Humming

Having a song in your heart (or your earphones) is one thing, but singing aloud stops a lot of people who feel they have to sound good or carry a tune. So if you're not ready to sing your way to the last row, you can still use a wonderful and more private kind of music to take you there.

Here's what to do: Inhale a full breath . . . and then exhale and hum all the way to the end of your breath. Yes, hum. You can hum with your eyes open or closed, although closing your eyes will give you a better and faster effect.

Make sure you hum louder than you're thinking. Hum as loud as you would sing in the shower. You can try different tones and volumes until you find the one that's sweetest to your ears—high-pitched, moderate, or deep—a tone that feels like you and that comes right from your center. When you find it, you'll feel your own vibration, as if chanting "om" in Zen meditation. Just keep inhaling deeply and humming on the exhale all the way to the end of your breath.

Do this for about a minute, or for about ten to fifteen breaths. The longer you can hum, the faster you'll quiet your mind, feel centered and relaxed, and move to the last row.

Belly Breathing

But, you know, if this doesn't suit you, you don't even need to hum. Several times in this book, I've mentioned that breathing is a "bridge" to the last row. Now I want to tell you about a most beautiful breathing bridge—call it the "Golden Gate"—that will connect you to your place of new perspectives and new solutions.

This special way of breathing I like to call "belly" breathing. It's the deep, slow abdominal breathing that has been taught by yoga masters from ancient times to help people develop calm and tranquility.

Try taking some belly breaths. Inhale through your nose to the count of four, letting your belly swell outward. Hold your breath for a count of four. Now exhale through your mouth to a count of four. Exhale completely—throw out all the air. Really push your breath as if blowing up a balloon. Feel and hear the "whoosh" of air as you exhale. Don't be concerned with what your stomach looks like or the loud sound of your exhale; this breathing is for your health. Wait a few seconds on the turning point, and begin again.

The four-beat timing is not fixed and final. As you practice belly breathing, you might want to hold your breath an extra beat or make the exhale double that of the inhale. Find a comfortable rhythm for yourself. If you start to feel a little dizzy, stop for a little while before continuing. Also, you don't need to breathe so deeply that your lungs burn. The whole experience should be soothing and relaxing.

In fact, just four or five good belly breaths trigger what Dr. Herbert Benson calls a "relaxation response," automatically lowering your heart rate, increasing your blood flow, and relaxing your muscles. Experts in relaxation like Dr. Benson say that if you take forty of these deep belly breaths every day your life will be healthier and you'll feel stronger, more filled with energy, more vital, and more open to life.

You'll also be spending more and more time in the last row, listening to your true, authentic inner voice.

Gibberish

Another means of expression that moves you quickly to the last row is the universal and special language called gibberish. You've spoken it before, although maybe not since you were a baby. At that time, in diapers, before you learned the outer language of your culture—and of your programming—you spoke your own personal inner language. It was an effortless flow of nonsense, of gibberish, and it calmed you, delighted you, helped you feel good, made you giggle, and quieted your mind.

Say this out loud: "Nika shopa woo noo" or "Hai chi wa na" or "Pi chika noh nay." That's gibberish, and if it was fun and calming to make those sounds, do it again. It feels right because it is right.

This may sound a little silly—and silly is good—but there's also a serious point. By speaking gibberish, you're learning to express yourself once again from your authentic center, in your true, intuitive voice, and it will help you clear your mind, get out of your own way, let go of stress, and maybe even laugh a little at yourself.

Make up your own gibberish, or use the samples above, but try speaking gibberish aloud (even if you just mumble it) for a minute or so whenever you feel stressed out or caught up in your challenge. Watch what happens. This is like cleaning out the cobwebs. When was the last time you've felt this relaxed, childlike, playful, and funny?

Laughter Is the Best Medicine

Laughing, finally, is one of the very shortest, easiest routes to the last-row perspective that I know of. A real belly laugh, from deep inside, is a magical thing. When you laugh wholeheartedly, with every cell of your body, your whole being is connecting with your inner voice and you end up feeling relaxed, peaceful, light, free, and at ease. This is a deep healing experience to have whenever possible. In fact, recent research (2009) at the University of Maryland School of Medicine has shown that laughter actually increases the flow of blood and oxygen to your heart and brain, thus protecting you from heart attacks and offsetting the effects of mental stress—and also lending strong scientific support to the old adage, laughter is the best medicine.

Now, singing and dancing take some know-how and practice. You might not feel comfortable doing these things. But laughing, giggling, even smiling are spontaneous, effortless. There's nothing to learn or to be good at. Laughter is a natural expression of joy in your heart . . . joy in your body . . . and joy for joy's sake.

Maybe the best place to start is with a smile. It doesn't even have to be a big smile on your face; it can be a subtle inner smile that spreads all over your body, and throughout your being. Try to feel this smile inside and you'll know what I mean, because it cannot be explained. Some people call it a "white light" from within that overwhelms them with joy. Others say it's like a small rose opening in their belly—very soft, delicate, and fragile, with the fragrance spreading all over their body.

It's impossible to explain because it's different for everybody. Certainly the freedom is tremendous. There is a feeling of oneness, wholeness, unity, and beauty.

And it's only a smile, not even a laugh; just a smile from your body, from your belly, your heart, your center.

Once you've felt this radiant inner smile, you can hold it inside and be happy for hours. And whenever you feel challenged, whenever you feel you're missing that happiness, just close your eyes and catch hold of your smile again—it's always there—and it will help you relax, get to the last row, and take the best care of yourself possible.

However, when your smile broadens and you break into a laugh—and it's total, like a full-body laugh that brings tears to your eyes—you quickly let go, accept, relax, and naturally connect with your true, authentic voice. Laughing lets you disappear and become your heart and soul. Laughing makes you feel light. It comes from your core. It centers you. When you laugh, there is no ego—the fifteenth-row Inner Critic vanishes! You're effortlessly in the last row with a loving awareness of the humor in life, and it's as if everything is flowing on its own.

Laughing makes all this happen so easily, so naturally. You don't need talent, practice, learning, or anything. It's not complex. It's the simplest thing in the world.

Comedy Tonight

Here's a Find Your Voice technique that can help you lighten up when you become seriously upset by your challenge.

Picture yourself in your inner theater, watching the movie of your life, and also watching your humorless, grim fifteenth-row Inner Critic as it watches the scene. Only this time, it's a movie you haven't seen before—this time, you're surprised and delighted to see that your movie is a comedy.

Maybe it's a slapstick comedy in which everything goes wrong in the craziest ways. Stressful situations, family frustrations, issues at work, worries, fears, and all the rest: Try to see them all from a comic point of view, with a twinkle in your eye. Just let yourself laugh, clown, mug for the camera, trip over your own feet, stumble and fall—let yourself go, and dive into your own imperfection.

Or better yet, have you seen those "blooper" shows on TV, or the outtakes added to some comedy DVDs? You know, clips showing the actors forgetting their lines or garbling words, and breaking each other up. Or the door sticks during the sketch, or the fake moustache comes unglued. And the actors come out of their roles, look at the camera, and dissolve in laughter.

Imagine your own blooper show of the comic "mis-takes" for your movie. Let yourself laugh at the lighter side of your challenge. Just be open and allow yourself to get the joke, see the humor, and enjoy yourself.

From the last row, you'll see a lot of comedy, even absurdity, in so many things we all do every day—in so many things we all take so seriously.

The End of All Our Exploring

In Step 3, you've been exploring the far edges of your experience: looking above and below, seeing outside and inside, embracing childhood and old age, writing good sense and speaking nonsense, drawing and dancing, inhaling and exhaling, crying and laughing. And the end of all this exploring? You arrive at the last row, where you find a new perspective on yourself and your life, where you see the bigger picture of your challenge, and where, most importantly, you come to know your true, authentic self, your deep intuition, the caring, compassionate, loving part of you that speaks of new solutions in your own wise, healing voice.

The modern American poet T. S. Eliot, who had dealt with an emotional challenge in his own life, expresses this very process in four profound and famous lines:

> We shall not cease from exploration
> And the end of all our exploring
> Will be to arrive where we started
> And know the place for the first time.

Squaw Peak

When speaking about the healing process, Milton Erickson was fond of telling the following magical coming-of-age story.

There's a place in Arizona called Squaw Peak. It's quite a big mountain, and just a couple of hundred years ago an Indian tribe lived down at the bottom, and a family of rattlesnakes lived way up at the top.

In the tribe at the bottom of Squaw Peak, there was a youngster who really wanted to be a grown-up, to be one of the adults. And so this young Indian would always ask, day after day, week after week, month after month, "When can I be grown up? When can I be an adult? When can I be one of you?" But, of course, the everyday things went on and on and on.

At the top of Squaw Peak, there was a young rattlesnake that really wanted to be accepted as one of the adult rattlesnakes and would always ask the adults, "When can I be one of you? When can I be an adult? When can I be grown up?" And, of course, the everyday things went on and on and on. That's just how things went.

And then one fateful day, the adult Indians at the bottom of Squaw Peak went to this young Indian and said, "Today is the day you can become an adult. All you have to do is climb to the top of Squaw Peak, and when you get there look around and find us a new place to live where there's sun, and shade, and water." And the young Indian could hardly wait and started to climb up Squaw Peak.

On the same fateful day, the adult rattlesnakes went to the young rattlesnake and said, "Today is the day. All you have to do to be an adult is go to the bottom of Squaw Peak, and when you get there look around and find us a new home where there's sun, and shade, and water." And the young rattlesnake started going right away.

About halfway up and halfway down, the young Indian and the young rattlesnake came face to face, eye to eye, staring at each other, moving around each other cautiously. And both of them realized that they could fight, and one may die, one may live, both may die, who knows? They stood there staring at each other for what felt like an eternity.

And after a long while, the young Indian started going back down Squaw Peak much slower than he walked up. The young rattlesnake started slithering back up Squaw Peak much slower than he had come down.

Finally, back down at the bottom of Squaw Peak, the young Indian told the adult Indians what happened in a sad, dejected, unhappy voice. And all of the adult Indians said together to this young Indian, "Welcome, you are now one of us. Self-respect is the most important thing."

And at the top of Squaw Peak when the rattlesnake finally got there, he told the adult rattlesnakes what had happened, and he was sad, dejected, and unhappy. But the adult rattlesnakes all at the same time said to the young rattlesnake, "Welcome, you are now one of us. Self-respect is the most important thing."

What's the point of the story? It's hard to say for sure, but clearly the story describes the life-changing power of two opposites meeting in the center. And it appears that in this fateful meeting something profound happens—some timeless voice is heard—telling the young Indian and the young rattlesnake of a new way to resolve their conflict. And, finally, the story suggests that for true growing up—for moving on in life, evolving, transcending your challenge—the most important thing is finding the intuitive wisdom to accept yourself, and to respect yourself, just the way you are.

So, whatever route or technique from Step 3 gets you there, when you arrive in the last row and listen quietly for a moment, here's in essence what your voice will tell you: Respect yourself, care for yourself, and even love yourself, without conditions, restrictions, or requirements. It's that simple. Once you start to respect and love yourself truly as you are, unconditionally, with all your strengths and weaknesses, you'll quickly discover how to resolve your challenge and evolve in your life.

Do this, and everything that's most important to you—your relationships, your achievements, your contributions, and all that you receive from life and from others—will bring you more joy than you thought possible.

CHAPTER 4

Voice Coaching

There's an old story about a young man rushing down a street in New York City with a violin case under his arm. He stops an old gentleman and frantically asks, "How do I get to Carnegie Hall?" The old man looks at the young man and somberly replies, "Practice, practice, practice."

Mastering the Find Your Voice process requires a little knowledge, and a lot of patience, commitment, trust . . . and practice. But the benefits are enormous and can bring about amazing changes in your life.

And it can work for everyone.

Still (and let's be honest), as you begin practicing the process, making it part of your life, you may well have questions and concerns, maybe even difficulties. Maybe you'll wonder about practical matters, such as the best times and places to work the three steps. Maybe you'll have trouble setting goals or maintaining your commitment. Or maybe you'll have process questions: about what to do, for instance, when you just can't accept your challenge, or express your Inner Judge, or get to the last row right away.

This is all normal, and it's going to happen, particularly when you're new at the process and haven't developed your Find Your Voice muscles very much. Expect questions and difficulties—they're part of the movie; they're part of the process; they're a completely natural thing.

I help my clients deal with these same issues (and more) almost daily. Acting as what you might call their voice coach, I answer their questions on how to get started and how to stay focused, I describe a number of techniques for navigating through rough times and getting back on track, and I offer tips and tweaks on how to practice the process most effectively, and thus how to reach their goals most efficiently.

Now I want to do the same for you.

Let's begin with the most common questions my clients ask on practical matters.

What's the First Thing I Should Do?

The first thing to do in the Find Your Voice process is to take a few minutes to state to yourself—and to write down in your journal—the specific goal you want to accomplish. Where *exactly* do you want this Find Your Voice inner work to take you? Giving yourself a detailed, well-defined goal is very important. Trying to work toward a vague or hazy objective can be like trying to see over the horizon through foggy binoculars. The clearer and more specific your goal, the more easily you'll see positive changes.

Thus, if your goal is to "lose weight," try to be more specific and spell out in detail what eating less would be like for you: No more snacking between meals, say, or taking a second helping at dinner, or eating sweets at night.

Here's another tip: Your Find Your Voice process will be more effective if you divide your overall goal into several smaller, more achievable goals. Particularly if your challenge has been a part of your life for a long time, you're better off making progress one small step at a time, one modest success leading to the next. Most of us can't drive a spike into a plank with one mighty blow, but we can do the job with many repeated taps.

Again, if your goal is to lose a good deal of weight (maybe fifty pounds or more), it's better to approach your long-range objective in smaller, intermediate steps, maybe three pounds a week, or fifteen pound in eight weeks. These are "doable" objectives, and the satisfaction of your small successes will strengthen your resolve to reach your larger goal.

How Often Should I Practice?

Daily practice is essential to developing your skill with the Find Your Voice process. It's helpful to recognize that the time you give to your practice is like gold you deposit in the bank of positive self-change. Even a small amount of time invested daily in your self-care quickly builds the balance in your inner personal account.

Ideally, you should do your three steps as close to your moment of challenge as possible. The sooner you deal with the stress of your pain, craving, fear, and so on, the sooner you'll relax, feel the shift, and find yourself again. You can do this once a day or many times a day, as needed.

But most people can't make time for this immediate response. In most cases, your busy life carries you along and you need to wait until later to do the process. Just make sure you don't put it off too long. If at all possible, try to complete the three steps some time that same day or night.

Daily practice is also vital in order to meet your long-range goals. More than just quelling a sudden craving or calming yourself down for the moment, you want to deal with your lifelong challenge: maybe losing weight (and keeping it off), or quitting smoking, or learning to manage your fear or your pain, or controlling your temper—whatever your challenge happens to be. Achieving these larger goals will take persistent, committed daily practice over time.

So either way, quick relief or long-term resolution, you need to make the time in your day, every day, to practice the Find Your Voice process.

When Should I Practice?

Let me say again: The very best time to practice is whenever you feel in the grip of your challenge. In other words, try to practice on an as-needed basis, whenever you most need yourself, all of yourself.

You might also find that practicing when you *aren't* in a crisis makes it a lot easier in the more critical times. For this pre-practice, try to set up a regular practice schedule. Developing a daily routine will weave the Find Your Voice process into the fabric of your life and help you remember your commitment.

There's no time of day that's right for everyone. You might find that early morning is best for you. It's often a quiet time in the house when you can gather your thoughts before the day's busyness. Or you might discover that midday is an ideal time. Midday is a rest point between morning and evening, and a time both to review the morning's experiences and to prepare for the balance of the day. Or you might find that just before bedtime is best. It's a time to breathe deeply and let go of the day's stress, helping you relax for a good night's sleep.

Now, if your life doesn't follow a regular schedule, or if you're the sort of person who can't stand routine, you might prefer to put off your practice until you feel like it. Just remember, you're making an investment in your self-care, and if you get in the habit of procrastinating, you can easily begin to skip sessions and shortchange your progress.

How Much Time Should I Spend Practicing?

It's very important that you don't feel you need to complete the Find Your Voice process quickly. There are a lot of self-help books out there these days promising a quick fix (*Happiness in 10 Minutes, Five Good Minutes,* and the like), but the time you need to resolve your challenge is uniquely your own. So take your time and proceed at your own pace.

Your practice time will in fact change as you learn the process and develop your inner power. When you begin, you might take thirty minutes to an hour to move through the three steps and deal with your stress. When you've become more skilled with the process, five to ten minutes a day might be just about right. When you've mastered the process, it will become like second nature, virtually automatic, and it will take you only a few moments to get to the last row, feeling relaxed and renewed.

One other point: Don't fall into the trap of spending *too* long doing this process. When you try too hard and spend hours a day doing the techniques, you can actually block your learning and impede your progress. In personal growth, you can easily encounter the law of diminishing returns.

A student once asked his Zen master how long he should meditate in order to find inner peace. The master answered, "Meditate one hour a day for one year." The student was eager and asked, "What if I meditate five hours a day?" The master answered, "Ah, then it will take you five years."

Should I Give Each Step Equal Time?

Not at all. The time you spend on the different steps will probably vary day to day. One day you might need more time for Step 1 (experiencing) and less time for Step 2 (judging), and then a different mix the next day. Just stay sensitive to your needs and flexible with your time.

Moreover, it's almost impossible to predict how long Step 3 (resolving) will take. Sometimes your creative last-row resolutions will surprise you, bubbling up spontaneously in just a few seconds, as though your intuition—your voice—can't wait to be heard. Other times, you can feel stuck (especially if you're trying too hard) and you may need to wait longer for a new idea or answer to come to you, and for the last-row shift to take place.

Where Should I Practice?

Doing the process on the spot, wherever your challenge confronts you, is best. But most often you'll need to find some other place to practice sometime later. Anywhere is fine, but try to choose a place that's comfortable, safe, and free from interruptions. And try to make it the *same* place as often as possible. Relaxation is the starting point for all of the techniques in this book, and finding a quiet, private, familiar place will help you relax.

If you choose a place outdoors, it should afford you peace and quiet. Better a secluded backyard or deck than a front porch where someone might bother you. When you're a bit more experienced and comfortable with the process, you might enjoy practicing in the warmth and freshness of a day at the beach, or sitting in a park.

However, to begin with, indoors will probably be better for most of you. At home, a quiet bedroom, office, or den might best suit you—especially if you have children. If it's hard to find privacy in your house, try sitting in your garage, maybe in your parked car (with the engine always off). If you're at work, close your office door and turn off the lights for a few minutes before your day begins or during your lunch hour.

Should I Sit or Lie Down?

Most people find that a relaxed sitting position is better than lying down. Lying down makes it too easy to drift off to sleep when you're in a very relaxed state of mind. Of course, if your challenge is insomnia, and your goal is going to sleep, then lying down is fine.

Select a comfortable chair—think of this as your "last-row" chair in your inner theater—with a high back that gives your head some support, or that allows you to sit upright. If your head is unsupported when you relax, it can easily roll back and startle you out of your inner focus. A pillow might help.

When you start your practice session, place your arms at your sides or on the arms of the chair if that's more comfortable, or let them relax in your lap. The most important thing is to be comfortable.

Should I Have My Eyes Open or Closed?

For most of you, having your eyes closed is best. Most people seem to close their eyes naturally when relaxing, probably because of the fatigue in their eyelids. So you're more comfortable with your eyes closed. But more importantly, as soon as you close your eyes you go inside, and it's there, inside, where you can more easily enter your inner theater and discover your inner wisdom.

All the same, many people skilled in the Find Your Voice process prefer to practice with their eyes open. If you keep your eyes open, you might want to fix your gaze upon some spot that has slow and regular movement, or no movement at all. Concentration is vital in your practice, and visual distractions can disturb your mental focus. It's a good idea to experiment practicing with your eyes open to see how well it works for you.

How Do I Deal with Distractions?

This is a commonly asked question: What do I do when irritating noises or other distractions break my concentration? Certainly, it can be difficult to stay relaxed and focused when a jet booms overhead, when a garbage truck clangs and rumbles by outside, or when your dog starts barking. No matter how well you've secluded yourself, nature and technology can intrude on your Find Your Voice practice.

When this happens, you don't have to fight or try to ignore the interruption. Besides, often the more you try to ignore something, the more you notice it. Instead of fighting the distraction, you can actually use it to deepen your relaxation. All that's required is a little imagination and you can re-frame the interruption and make it part of your practice.

For instance, the noise of a garbage truck outside might suggest throwing away your tension and stress. You might tell yourself, "As the sound of the garbage truck approaches, I can place all my tensions and worries into a big black trash bag. When the truck stops at my house, I can pitch the bag into the truck to be hauled away to the dump."

While visualizing this, imagine your trash bag being swallowed up in the huge garbage truck bed and driven away from you. Feel the relaxing of tension and pressure as the sound of the truck rolls on past your house and slowly retreats out of hearing.

There's no limit to what your imagination can do to turn stressors into relaxers. Here are some more examples:

The sound of a leaf blower next door reminds me that all my worries can be blown away for a little while.

My dog barking makes me think of a beautiful park where all dogs run free, and where I'm relaxing on a rock by the lake.

A clock ticking reminds me of my heart beating steadily. I can calm my heart with my breathing and unwind from the hectic pace of the day.

A jetliner droning overhead makes me think of all the wonderful places people fly for a relaxing vacation. I'll just float along with them for a while.

With suggestions such as these, you can use outside distractions to help you relax and refocus on your practice.

How Can I Quiet My Mind?

Distractions can also come from inside. For instance, people who think a great deal have trouble turning off their minds. Their thoughts can be like cars crisscrossing at a busy intersection or like voices overlapping at a cocktail party. If you find you have so many thoughts in your head that you can't easily relax and get into your Find Your Voice practice, try the following technique for quieting your mind with awareness, acceptance, and expression.

First, focus on your thoughts. Notice how they come into your mind, stay a while, and then depart. Observe how you can separate your thoughts and listen to them one at a time. Identify one thought, then another, and another, and so on.

Don't challenge your thoughts or reject them, and certainly don't try to ignore them. The idea is not to create any conflict over your thoughts, but to allow them, welcome them, and make them your point of focus for the time being.

Let your thoughts happen and use them in a counting exercise.

Start counting your thoughts. Begin at one and count up to forty or fifty—count them all. Become very good at counting your thoughts. Make sure you separate them so you don't count only one thought when there are really three bound together. Count carefully and accurately and notice how many different thoughts you have. Then begin breathing slowly and regularly to a pattern of counting. Maybe breathing in on each thought and exhaling with a different thought.

In a short while, you'll notice how absorbed you've become in the process of counting your thoughts, and you'll find yourself deeply relaxed, focused, and ready for your Find Your Voice practice session.

How Can I Calm My Emotions?

Some people can be so wrapped up in strong emotions—sadness, anger, guilt, worry, and so forth—that they can't relax. If you feel your emotional state is blocking you as you begin your practice, you might try this technique for calming your heart, once again through greater awareness, acceptance, and expression.

Start by getting as comfortable as possible. Find a place to be alone for a little while, and close your eyes while taking several deep slow breaths . . .

Focus on the emotion or emotions you're feeling at the present moment. Ask yourself, "What am I feeling, right now?" Don't try to change or get rid of your feelings. We are primarily emotional beings, so there's no sense in trying to talk yourself out of feelings that have you in their grip.

Let's say you're tensed up with worry. Try to look in detail at your worry—even exaggerate your worry—to become aware of the feeling as fully as possible.

Next, picture the worry as a place you're approaching—a house, or a cave, or a thicket of trees. Become aware of the entrance to your worry; focus on how the worry comes upon you or how you enter into the emotion.

Once inside with your worry, listen to the voice of your worry. No trying to change anything; just observe and listen to gain more awareness. You can even show understanding and compassion for the worried part of you. Make that part of you a friend. Then begin exiting the place of worry together.

Take several deep and cleansing breaths—breathe in a cool focus on your inner friend, and breathe out your worry. Take four or five deep breaths to let go, and you'll find your worry has helped you relax into your practice.

Why Is Visual Imagery So Important?

The language of the intuition is the language of visual imagery. So, if you want to communicate effectively with your last-row self, you'll need to learn a little about how to "speak" with visual imagery.

What's visual imagery? A visual image is simply a mental picture. Close your eyes and recall the first thing you saw when you got up this morning. Or picture what your car looks like. Or imagine your favorite color. In order to tell me any of these things, you had to "re-member" them, that is, reshape them in your imagination and see them as a picture with your mind's eye. This is using imagery. "The soul never thinks without a picture," said Aristotle.

Without a doubt, visual imagery—the creation of the imagination—is a powerful tool in the Find Your Voice process.

Your unconscious mind recognizes and responds to mental pictures much more readily than it does to abstract words and ideas. So by using imagery, you're able to speak with greater clarity and richness to your intuition and thus develop a deeper level of communication with your true, authentic self.

What If I Have Trouble Visualizing?

All of us have the ability to communicate with imagery, but not all of us are very fluent with the language. So let's take a moment at this point to sharpen up your visualizing skills.

Here are some easy-to-use visualization exercises of the type devised by Michael Samuels, MD, author of *Seeing with the Mind's Eye,* and the foremost expert in using guided imagery for mind-body healing.

1 Gaze at one of the geometrical shapes below. Then shut your eyes and try to visualize it.

2 Examine for a few moments a three-dimensional object in your home or workplace, such as an orange, a glass of water, or a lamp. Close your eyes and imagine the object.

3 Visualize a schoolroom from your elementary school, or how you got to school as a child.

4 Visualize your house or your apartment, room by room.

⑤ Visualize a person you know, from their eyes to their smile.

⑥ Visualize your own reflection in a mirror.

Practice these exercises for a few minutes every day for three or four weeks, even after you've begun your Find Your Voice practice. It won't take you much more time than it takes to read these instructions. You might be surprised at how vivid and creative your imagery can become. You'll also be opening up a direct line of communication with your intuition.

Expand these exercises with different people, places, and objects, particularly those that come from within *you*—your favorite images called up from your memories and experiences.

This practice is vital for your success. Many of the techniques in this book ask you to see with your mind's eye in this way. But even more importantly, your ability to visualize images allows you to see your life movie on-screen and your Critic sitting in the fifteenth row of your inner theater.

Visualization or Meditation?

Imagining scenes on your inner movie screen is what I call "creative visualization," and it's a powerful method for going deep inside your unconscious mind and getting in touch with your wise, healing inner Voice.

Creative visualization has much in common with meditation. Both begin with breathing and mental imagery to calm and center the mind. And both strive to help you heighten your inner awareness, letting you become a detached observer of your thoughts and feelings.

But there are two important differences. First, creative visualization goes beyond awareness and taps into the healing power of acceptance and expression. You don't just passively observe your thoughts and feelings; you move on to embracing them and letting them go.

And second, creative visualization is more goal-directed than meditation. In creative visualization you focus personal, healing imagery on your specific physical or emotional challenge: anything from stress management to pain relief, easing of fear and anxiety, weight loss, improved performance in business or sports, mind-body healing, and many, many more.

Classic meditation is a wonderful practice, and heightened inner awareness is a valuable starting point in the Find Your Voice process. But creative visualization is more comprehensive and proactive, closer to what might be called *guided* meditation.

What Do I Do When My Commitment Wavers?

You're going to have times in the Find Your Voice process when your commitment wavers and you feel as though it's not worth going on. Maybe you'll feel stuck in committee, or stuck in the fifteenth row, and you'll feel the mountain is just too high to climb. When it all seems like too much and you feel like giving up, here's something to try:

The way things start is usually the way they go, so when you wake up in the morning, be aware of your determination—your deep intention—to achieve your goal. Lie still in your warm, half-conscious state, and for five to ten minutes before you get up, be aware of, accept, and express your deep commitment to yourself. Visualize, think, and feel yourself making healthy choices, handling difficult situations beautifully, with relaxation, self-confidence, and self-love, and feeling optimistic about your whole day's success with your goal. Breathe deeply several times, and then on the last breath just before you get up for the day, state to yourself on the inhale, "I will do it . . . I am fully committed to my health and happiness," pause, and then on the exhale say your name.

Then that night when you go to bed, be aware of your deep determination to accomplish your goal. When you lie down in bed, review your day, focusing on what was right about your actions, your choices, your attitude, your awareness, acceptance, and expression. Be aware of your goal for five to ten minutes, breathe deeply several times, and as you relax and become drowsy on an inhale just before you drop off to sleep, say to yourself silently, "I will do it . . . I am fully committed to my health and happiness," pause, and then on the exhale say your name.

Do this for a few days, whenever you feel your commitment lagging. Add it into your wake-up and bedtime routines. And in a matter of two or three days, you'll observe a significant change.

Doesn't Acceptance Mean Giving Up?

It's easy to think "accepting" means giving up or resigning yourself to your problems. But, in fact, the opposite is true. Accepting yourself is a *positive* action; it's proactive, energizing, and life-changing—it creates momentum, it opens doors. As soon as you accept yourself just as you are, positive changes begin to happen.

In my study of meditation, I came across an intriguing saying: "Acceptance is transcendence." This means that whenever you accept something in life you immediately start to transcend it, to evolve past it, to rise above it.

Once you've experienced the positive energy of acceptance, and made it your new habit, you might be amazed at your progress. Later on today when you feel angry at yourself (and you will), you might accept that a part of you feels angry. Then the next day when you start to feel hopeless about your progress (and you will), you might accept that a part of you feels hopeless.

And this will spread to other parts of your life. When something difficult or stressful happens, you'll accept it. Then when the stress disappears, you'll accept that, too. When you feel good, you'll accept it. Then when the good feeling goes away, you'll accept that as well.

You'll not be trying to change anything, fix anything, or get rid of anything. You'll not be insisting on having only certain thoughts and feelings, those you *should* have. You'll be observing and accepting all your thoughts and feelings just as they are.

As I've said before, you're not going to get rid of your thoughts and feelings anyway. Your thoughts and feelings—all of them, good and bad, positive and negative—are organic parts of you, like your fingers and toes. They've grown and developed with you through all the ages and stages of your life, as you've learned how to deal with different problems and different people.

When your fingers or toes are hurt or you bruise them, you don't cut them off and try to get rid of them. You decide to take better care of yourself and heal them, and this lets you move more freely and handle things better.

By accepting yourself just as you are, you're learning to do the same thing with your thoughts and feelings.

What If I Just Can't Accept Something about Myself?

Okay, this gets pretty paradoxical, but there's no other way to talk about it. Maybe you've come down hard on yourself and have defined something you think, feel, or do as unacceptable, terrible, or shameful. What can you do? Well, first, don't keep fighting it by *trying* to accept it. That only traps you in a vicious circle of resisting your resistance.

Instead, do the opposite: Step back and *accept that you can't accept it*. In other words, dive right into your feeling of resistance, ride the current until you're out of it, until you're free of it and have settled into an accepting state of mind. Once your mind relaxes into acceptance mode, it will be much easier for you to get through to the last row and watch your whole inner battle with more friendliness, caring, and compassion.

You see, when you accept your resistance, you automatically begin to accept your Inner Judge. All your resistance —skepticism, pessimism, negativity—comes from your Inner Judge, and you really don't want to fight this part of yourself. Because you'll never win! But when you accept your Inner Judge and work *with* it instead of *against* it, you quickly soften this negative voice in your head and begin to untangle the knot of your resistance.

Does My Inner Judge Also Make Positive Criticism?

Yes, occasionally. Your Inner Judge never stops giving its opinions, and some of its judgments are bound to be positive or approving.

Many times, however, your Inner Judge's positive criticism is only a sly way of setting you up for a fall. For instance, you might congratulate yourself on earning a big bonus at work, or buying an expensive car, or playing a great round of golf. But this almost immediately invites negative criticism in by the back door. Self-congratulation is ego based and your ego is never satisfied with you or your success. Even as you pat yourself on the back, your ego will try to find fault and tear you down, whispering of inadequacy ("You were lucky"), of unworthiness ("You don't deserve this"), and of impatience ("Well, it's about time").

As always, go ahead and listen to these judgments—positive or negative—but then get to the last row where you can see your success with more wisdom and hear the voice of joy and gratitude rather than of self-praise.

Are There Other Ways of Expressing My Challenge?

Yes. Sometimes it helps to get physical:

If you belong to a gym or club, if you work out at home, or if you jog or walk in your neighborhood, you can use your exercise routine to help you express your challenge. "Exercise" in Latin means "to throw off restraints," and so, whatever troubling thoughts, feelings, worries, or concerns you're holding inside, you can really let them go, express them, as you lift weights, run, swim, cycle, and so forth.

Other times, you might even have to fight to let go of your feelings:

Have a special old pillow at home, or maybe use a punching bag in your garage or at your gym. When you're feeling really stressed, get hold of your pillow or bag, and for ten minutes punch it as hard as you can, really whale on it, kick it, smack it, throw it. Be aware of all your thoughts and feelings in your head and your heart, and just let them all go. All the anger, sadness, frustration, fear, shame—whatever stress you're feeling that day, or maybe that you've been feeling for years. If you have some privacy, shout, sob, scream. Hold nothing back. If people are around, just shout it all inside your head.

Then for ten minutes more, sit silently, breathe, and relax deeply. Love your whole self. It's time to let yourself understand that freedom is the goal and that awareness, acceptance, and expression are what get you there.

Also, you can express your challenge using this sort of creative visualization:

Imagine all your worries, frustrations, negative thoughts and feelings packed tightly into a small, stuffy, sour-smelling room. Imagine yourself opening a window in that room. A fresh breeze blows in, so clear and cool it opens all your senses, and all the negatives swirl and drift out into the fresh air. Take three deep, satisfying breaths and relax.

The Big Red Hot-Air Balloon

Here's an extended creative visualization—it's a favorite of many of my clients—for letting go of all the mental and emotional baggage you've been carrying around inside all day, or all your life. Picture this scene and let your imagination be as playful as you want.

You're taking a walk outdoors in a beautiful grassy field. You can feel the sun shining and feel its warmth on your body, a slight cool breeze blowing by, the grasses bending just enough to be beautiful and graceful, and the birds floating and soaring in the bright blue sky. And you notice there's a beautiful meadow off to the right, and sitting in the middle of the meadow is a great big red hot-air balloon—and it grabs your attention. Like a little kid, you wonder about it. It's kind of weird to see such a great big red hot-air balloon in the middle of a meadow. So maybe you're curious and maybe you're surprised (it really doesn't matter), but you want to see it up close.

You walk down to this great big red hot-air balloon, and as you get closer to it, you see it has a big basket under it—you know, the kind you can ride in. There's no one in the basket, so you look inside and see there's a big empty burlap gunnysack on the floor. It's almost as if the gunnysack was put there for you to load in all your unfinished business, any stress, any problems, any challenges that have been in your life.

And so you start filling the gunnysack with your negative thoughts, your guilt, stress, troubles, worries, just filling it and filling it, old stuff, new stuff, current stuff, past stuff, little stuff, big stuff, getting the stress out of your chest, the guilt out of your head, the worry out of your stomach. And as you're filling the gunnysack, you start feeling lighter and more comfortable. And the more stuff you put in, the better you feel, until the sack is all full. And when it's all full, and you've heaved it back into the basket, you start to feel really better and more comfortable and relieved and kind of happy about this amazing opportunity that you've discovered.

And then you notice there are sandbags holding the big red hot-air balloon to the ground, tied to the basket by thick pieces of rope. But you see a knife nearby and with it you start to cut the sandbags loose. So you cut the first sandbag loose, and when you do, you feel like you're letting go, cutting the cords to the stress, and the worry, and the hassles. And this is a great feeling. And then you go to the next piece of rope and the next sandbag and you cut that one and you feel even better, like you're really letting go, feeling really free and comfortable. And you go to the next one, cut that one loose, and now this great big red hot-air balloon is starting to lift a little bit off the ground and that feels even better. And you go all the way around, and you cut all the sandbags loose, and you really feel like you're letting go, once and for all, of all that unfinished stuff you put in the gunnysack.

And when you get to the last rope, and cut the last sandbag loose, naturally all your stress and negativity start lifting up and away from you as this great big red hot-air balloon starts lifting into the sky. And as it leaves the ground, you have a great, comfortable feeling of letting go and releasing. And as it floats higher in the sky, you feel even better. You may even feel like waving good-bye—it just feels so good to see all that stress, and worry, and guilt, and difficulty floating away.

And the higher it gets, the better you feel. The higher it soars, the lighter and freer you feel. And pretty soon that great big red hot-air balloon is just a red circle in the blue sky, and it keeps getting higher and higher and farther and farther away and you feel lighter and freer and more relaxed, happy. Pretty soon, it's just a little red dot in the great big blue sky. And then it's gone, vanished.

It's great feeling free, relaxed, and happy, knowing how to let go, how to feel better anytime, anyplace, with this great big red hot-air balloon. You can do this every day, for a couple of minutes, for ten minutes, two minutes. It really doesn't matter. It's a great way to release your challenge and take the best possible care of yourself.

Do I Always Have to Do the Three Steps in Sequence?

Not at all. The Find Your Voice process can be a straight march, 1-2-3, but it can also be more back-and-forth. The reality is, as you practice the process, you'll probably find that you need to loop back on occasion, revisiting steps that feel incomplete. You've heard of "two steps forward, one step back"? Well, after Step 1 and Step 2, you might feel you need to go back and do more of Step 1 (experiencing)—maybe more accepting or more expressing—before you're able to move back to Step 2 and then on to Step 3. Thus, your route might be 1-2-1-2-3, or maybe something even more complicated.

Just remember: Whatever route you take, make sure that you always finish up at Step 3, in the last row.

What's important is that you stay flexible, keep the process fluid, and take the time you need. As you practice, you'll develop a sure sense of when you've finished with one step and are ready to move on to the next. Trust yourself here.

How Long Will It Take for This to Work?

One of your greatest difficulties will be dealing with your impatience to see results. The Find Your Voice process will always help you in the moment with your challenge, and yet long-term resolution can take weeks, months, or years, depending on how long you've been living with your challenge, and how well you're holding to your commitment to the process.

Remember that change is part of nature, and also part of your own human nature. Milton Erickson told me many times that "Everyone is an individual in a process of development." In this book, I've tried to define this process of development and explain how it works in just three steps, and yet there's always a learning curve in something this powerful. Changing your life, growing as a person, takes time, and nothing can be done faster than you can integrate. When you've integrated new learning, your capabilities expand and then you can work on integrating more. That's how it goes.

Personal growth is not like seasonal blossoms. It's like redwood trees that take hundreds of years to grow. You're growing new roots and they go deep into the earth. Like a redwood tree, you grow deep down into the earth and you also grow a hundred feet up into the sky. You're deeply rooted in the earth, and you're also reaching for the stars and connecting with the clouds. It doesn't take a few weeks like a seasonal flower. It's not like a dream that comes and goes. It's not pretend. It doesn't always come fast, but it lasts. Enjoy growing tall and strong, like a redwood tree. Give yourself the time you need. Work playfully and with your inner wisdom. Be patient with your whole self; patience is a mark of progress.

There's no rush and there's no skipping steps. Impatience is not from the last row—it's not true to you. Impatience shows that you want to impose yourself, to control everything, that you want everything right now. Impatience means "My willpower should fix everything." From your new learning, you know that this is your critical, judgmental fifteenth-row perspective.

You're also learning that patience is one of the greatest gifts you can give yourself. Patience enhances everything: relationships, health, success, and personal freedom. Patience means you don't try to push the river to make it go faster. Just the opposite: You go with the flow of the river, and you trust that you'll get to your goal. Patience means that you'll relax, be aware, accept, let go, trust, and have hope; it means that you'll not lose heart, and that you'll do everything you can—be 100 percent true to yourself—to grow as a person on a daily basis. From your new learning, you know that this is your unconditionally loving last-row perspective.

Naturally, you're learning that this is a paradox and may even feel like a miracle: The less you force things to hurry, the more quickly they happen; and the more you try to force things, the longer it takes.

Just breathe in and say the word "patience" to yourself. Then breathe out and say your first name to yourself. Do this for ten to fifteen full breaths. Wake up in the morning with this, and do this five to ten times during your day. You can do this in the middle of a stressful situation. You can do this at bedtime, too.

This breath work is your bridge to the last row, your connection to the true, authentic, intuitive voice of your inner wisdom.

Taekwondo

Almost all my new clients ask me for a real-life example of how the whole three-step Find Your Voice process works. So, to end as I began, on a personal note, here's the story of how I coached one of my daughters through a small but stressful crisis in her young life.

My daughter was twelve years old and had been studying the martial art Taekwondo for several years. Though not a very aggressive child, she dearly wanted to earn her black belt. Doing so required going to a competition to spar (it felt like "fighting" to her) with kids she didn't know and who generally had more experience. With trepidation in her heart, she and I went together, father and daughter, filing into the event with probably a couple thousand other kids and parents.

As the competition progressed, she was miserable and performing with more fear than confidence. She didn't want to hurt anyone. She didn't want to be there, didn't want to spar. She was having trouble putting her learned skills into action against girls who were bent on winning. Resisting competition was going to get in the way of her reaching her full potential with something she loved.

Now, to help all my kids get through the normal challenges of childhood, I had taught them some simple breathing techniques and the basics of the Find Your Voice process. We had made it into a family game, dubbing it, affectionately, "Going to the Movies."

So, right in the middle of the Taekwondo event, I knelt down beside my daughter and said, "Honey, let's 'go to the movies.'" I asked her, "How are you feeling right now? What's happening on your movie screen?" (Step 1).

She replied, "I want to go home. I hate this."

"Good," I prompted. "What else?"

"Why do I have to do this? Can't I just skip this part?"

"No honey, it's necessary to accept and express your feelings if you're to get past them. Just go ahead and say what you're feeling."

She spilled it all out. "This competition is dumb. I hate it. I'm doing horribly and I'm so embarrassed."

Between you and me, the event *was* intense. Almost any kid who wasn't cutthroat aggressive could have related to what she was experiencing. I was grateful that I was there to serve as her sounding bound. (Whenever I do the Going to the Movies steps myself, I do my feelings check-in silently, write them in a journal with my non-dominant hand, or go for a solo walk, or drive and talk to myself.)

Next, I whispered to my daughter that she might want to go to the fifteenth row and hear what her Inner Critic was saying about her and the competition (Step 2). This is the number-one place where athletes, both amateur and professional, get stuck. Learning at twelve or forty-two or any age to accept and express your Inner Judge/Critic moves you from barely coping to creatively transcending that which routinely hobbles your life.

My daughter opened up and relayed the browbeating she was receiving from her fifteenth-row Critic: "You should be able to do this. Your Taekwondo teacher is here with his wife; they thought you'd be good at this. What are the other kids thinking? They think you're being a baby. Their parents probably think so, too." Saying this aloud released a load of stress.

Just think how different it would've been had I barked, "Go on! Stop being scared and go for it!" Without venting her feelings and admitting her judgments, she would have been in an even greater muddle and would have written me off as another stress agent pressing her to perform. Instead, these two steps freed her to make the master move in the Find Your Voice process.

So, I asked my open-minded, open-hearted twelve-year-old to go into the last row of the theater (Step 3). Her eyes closed as she focused her imagination, picturing herself sitting in the last row, watching the movie screen and also the fifteenth-row Critic, feeling all the feelings and hearing all the judgments from this calm, distant, loving perspective—and asking herself, "What's the best way to deal with what's going on?"

"Do the breathing," I coaxed my daughter. (I could tell she was straining a bit, so I had her return to Step 1 for a moment.) Her eyes closed again as commotion from the sparring matches roared in the exhibition hall. We slipped into our own little world. "Accept your breath *as it is*," I said. "Inhale 'acceptance.'" Her lungs expanded. Exhaling, she mouthed her name. Her body began to relax. After a few breaths, she started remembering that she enjoyed—and was really good at—practicing Taekwondo moves with her friends in her local studio. Her once-tight face eased as her fears subsided.

Now, in the last row, my daughter told me she understood that all she had to do was focus on the moves she had worked on so hard, and engage in each sparring match as if "I was having fun with my friends." And even more importantly, she said she understood that she just needed "to do my best" and "not be mad at myself," no matter how she did in her matches.

Wow! There it was. This insight, this new understanding, was the gift of her intuition, of her true, authentic self. She had resolved her problem on her own in just minutes, and was ready to get back into the competition.

So how did my daughter do in the sparring? Newly relaxed and confident, she went from having virtually no points to placing first in her division. Together we celebrated, each a different victory.

Helping yourself win through your own crisis in life, no matter how great or small the challenge, is a skill that each of you can develop. Your best decisions and answers are waiting within, but tapping into them, particularly during times of duress, requires that you experience your challenge, judge your challenge, and then get yourself to the last row, where you can resolve your challenge through the loving, caring voice of your inner wisdom.

Each of you has this same chance to achieve some extraordinary change in your life. My fondest hope is that you'll take from this book a new confidence, an exhilarating and empowering certainty that now, using the 1-2-3 Find Your Voice process, you'll know (from deep down inside) how to meet your challenge and reach your life's goals.

Index

expressing your thoughts and feelings for, 26, 27–28, 29
unfinished business with, 25, 26
Parent trap, 67, 68
Past, embracing your, 109, 110, 111
Patience, 161
Physical challenges, dealing with
    step 1: experience your challenge, 9
    step 2: judge your challenge, 9, 10
    step 3: resolve your challenge, 10, 11
Pineal gland, 101
Pornography addiction, challenge of, 59

R

Racehorse technique, 78, 79, 80
"Relaxation response," 127
Repression, emotional, role in creating personal challenges, 5
Resolving your challenge, 89–136
Rock and roll technique, 124, 125
Ruiz, Don Miguel, 60, 61, 64
Rumi, Jalal ad-Din, 54, 56, 57

S

Samuels, Dr. Michael, 149
"Sati," 78
Say your name exercise, 33, 34
"Seat of the soul," 101
Seeing with the Mind's Eye, 149
Self-judgment, origin of, 67
Sense of humor, engaging your, 98, 99
Seven senses, 97, 98, 99
Should's, case of, 16, 17
"Sixth chakra," 101
"Sixth sense." See Intuition
Song and dance technique, 123, 124–125, 126
"Sorcerer's Apprentice, The," 87
Squaw Peak, 132, 133, 134
Stress, role in our lives, 5
"Superego," 60

T

Taking your judge for a walk, 84, 85, 86
"Teacher inside," 100
Tension
    being aware of, 39, 40
    diving into, 42, 43

"Tenth gate," 101
The Power of Now, 61
Turning points, 31, 32
Third eye, 100, 101, 102
Thoughts and feelings, repressed, 35, 36
Time traveling, 107, 108, 109
Tolle, Eckhart
    and the "ego," 61
    and Inner Judge, 64
Tree rings, and person's past, 29, 30
TruSage
    and the Committee Meeting, 46
    definition of, 4
Turning points for breathing, 31, 32

U

"Unconscious," 4
Unfinished business with parents, 25, 26
University of Maryland School of Medicine study, and laughter, 129

V

Visual imagery
    communicating with, 149, 150
    importance of, 148, 149
Visualization
    importance of, 148, 149
    or meditation, 150, 151
    trouble with, 149, 150

W

Weight, losing, and Find Your Voice process, 139
White light, 129
"Wise passiveness," 78
"Wizard of Phoenix," 2, 3, 4
Wordsworth, William, 78

Y

Yeats, W.B., 4
Yin and yang, 51–53

Z

Zen meditation, 78

About the Authors

Brian Alman, PhD, is the world's leading authority on mind-body healing, wellness, and self-care. In private practice for over thirty years, he has coached and trained more than ten thousand people in his simple yet powerful self-healing techniques. Also, through Dr. Alman's companies, TruSage™ and Mental Fitness™, as well as his books, speaking engagements, TV and radio appearances, CDs, videos, and websites, he has reached hundreds of thousands more people and helped them resolve their challenges and achieve amazing personal and professional growth. For more information, go to www.TruSage.com, where you'll find a complete biography, published studies on the success of Dr. Alman's work, as well as special recordings and downloads designed to accompany *The Voice*.

Dr. Stephen Montgomery, PhD, has since 1988 been the editor-in-chief of Prometheus Nemesis Book Company, the publishers of Dr. David Keirsey's works on personality types. In 1978 Dr. Montgomery edited Keirsey's *Please Understand Me*, and he was also the editor and co-writer of Keirsey's 1998 *Please Understand Me II*. Dr. Montgomery's own books are *The Pygmalion Project* and *People Patterns: A Modern Guide to the Four Temperaments*. Dr. Montgomery has worked with Brian Alman for twenty years and was the co-writer of Dr. Alman's most recent book, *Keep It Off: Your Keys to Weight Loss for Life*.